Animal Tracks
Activity Guide

Written and compiled by Michele Roest
Edited by Julie Lalo

Activity Guide

is copublished by:

National Wildlife Federation
1400 16th Street NW
Washington, DC 20036

and

NEA Professional Library
National Education Association
P.O. Box 509
West Haven, CT 06516-9904

The National Wildlife Federation is the nation's largest conservation education organization whose mission is to educate, inspire, and assist individuals and organizations of diverse cultures to conserve wildlife and other natural resources and to protect the Earth's environment in order to achieve a peaceful, equitable, and sustainable future.

William W. Howard, President and CEO
Lynn Greenwalt, Vice President, Conservation Programs and Special Assistant to the President
Cheryl K. Riley, Vice President, Educational Outreach
Lista Lincoln, Animal Tracks On-Line Education Program Director
Elenor Hodges, Animal Tracks Education Program Assistant

Note: The opinions expressed in this book should not be construed as representing the policy or position of the National Education Association. Materials published by the NEA Professional Library are intended to be discussion documents for educators who are concerned with specialized interests of the profession.

NWF: ISBN 0-945051-59-X
NEA: ISBN 0-8106-1872-9

Design provided by SUPON DESIGN GROUP, Washington, D.C.

Animal art by original *Animal Tracks* artist and creator Susan Morrison.

Production Staff: Marti Burton, Melissa Murray, Charlene Vivian, Scherrie Bussineau, Earlene Edwards, Fred Cornelius

The text was printed on processed chlorine-free recycled paper with 20 percent post-consumer waste. No chlorine was added in the manufacturing process.

The chlorine used to bleach paper to its typical bright whiteness combines with organic material in paper mill wastes to form contaminants that pollute waters and are toxic to humans, fish and wildlife. One of the things that you can do to reduce the buildup of toxic chemicals in humans and wildlife is to buy and use chlorine-free paper.

Contents

Animal Tracks

All living things share the same basic needs of food, clean water and shelter. The natural resources, physical processes, plants and animals on Earth have provided us with everything necessary to live a quality life on this planet. For thousands of years, we've enjoyed food, space and shelter, as well as air supplied and cleaned by green plants and a naturally maintained water purification system. As the human population continues to grow and use natural resources in a way that depletes their reserves, we face the loss of the very things that we need to live.

Humans are clearly the smartest and most advanced of all animals. But, in some ways, our ability to think intellectually can be a problem. We're apparently the only species able or willing to ignore the effect nature has on our lives.

Seemingly, it's only when disasters occur that we are forced to acknowledge that nature works according to its own laws, and that, despite our knowledge and advancement, we must still bow to the endless power of the natural world.

At this moment, we face one of the greatest disasters ever known to humanity: the destruction of the diversity and abundance of life on Earth. With the loss of this diversity and abundance, we also lose some of our own abilities to survive and reproduce. No technology exists to replace what we have lost — we can only try to preserve what we still have. Instead of trying to control the processes of nature, we are challenged to use our powerful problem-solving skills to find ways to meet our own human needs while still preserving the bounty of life on Earth. That is the inherent goal of *Animal Tracks*.

Follow the Animal Tracks

All mammals show tremendous similarity to one another. We are warm-blooded, give birth to living young and feed them milk from our own bodies. All animals with backbones (vertebrates) share a similar body structure. We have two front appendages and two hind ones. The foot and wing structure of many animals have five digits, just as human hands and feet do.

The *Animal Tracks Activity Guide* strives to reinforce the connection we all have to nature and to the ways our world functions. It offers activities that illustrate life's processes and how humans and other living things respond to these processes. The lessons are designed to explain a scientific concept, present a conservation issue of concern or provide opportunities for students to use their own skills at solving the complex environmental issues that we face. When using this guide, be sure to emphasize the similarities we share with other animals, and the opportunities we have to learn from them.

Animal Tracks Activity Guide

About the Animal Tracks Activity Guide

- The *Animal Tracks Activity Guide* is coordinated with *Animal Tracks* (the children's book), although both can work independently of each other. Having extra copies of *Animal Tracks* for your students will help reinforce the concepts and ideas presented in the *Activity Guide*.

- The *Activity Guide* contains 11 units, each concentrating on a different conservation issue. All activities in a unit can be used to thoroughly explore a topic. Or, choose just a few to augment a pre-existing lesson plan.

- Emphasis is placed on critical thinking and interpretation. Hypothesis testing, experimentation, analysis and discussion are used extensively. Role play and group work are emphasized as well.

- The activities are designed to meet current curriculum standards, and are multidisciplinary, hands-on and outcome-based. Science concepts are stressed, but all subject areas are covered in the *Activity Guide*.

- Learning objectives stated at the start of each activity allow teachers to check for cognitive understanding of the concepts.

- Activities are written for the 4th- to 6th-grade level, but all include modifications and extensions that allow teachers to adjust the lessons to meet the specific needs of the class.

- The *Challenge* defines and directs the focus of each unit. *Did You Know* offers "clues" to understanding the challenges, either by reinforcing them or by providing information useful in finding solutions. You may wish to copy this page and post it on the wall while your class is studying the topic.

- Each of the activities in the units includes a *Background* section, which contains specific information and facts pertinent to that activity. The *Background* section can be read aloud as a way to introduce the activity.

- Reproducible black line handouts are provided with many lessons, and include a teacher's version where appropriate. The *Glossary* contains definitions for the words listed in the *Vocabulary* sections of the lessons.

Key

Indicates ready-to-copy activity sheets for students that supplement the activities.

Indicates teacher's version of activity sheets with answers.

Backyard Wildlife

The Challenge

As we build cities, factories and homes in what used to be wild areas, we displace the wild animals and plants that lived there. Wild animals and plants play an important role in the natural balance of the world. We can repair some of the effects of development by creating places for wildlife in our backyards, school grounds and empty lots, and by learning about living side-by-side with nature.

Did You Know?

• All living things share the same basic requirements of food, water, shelter and open space. There is a limited supply of these things on earth.

Chart: We're Growing Fast Where should we all live?

World Population

2.5 billion	4.4 billion	5.2 billion	8.5 billion (predicted)
1950	1980	1990	2025

Every day, some of these human beings move into places where only plants and animals used to live.

• The need for timber used in construction creates demand for trees. In many areas, when diverse forests are cut down, they are replaced with only one species of tree. The result is destruction of the complex ecosystem that existed before.

• In neighborhoods, cats and dogs that chase rabbits, squirrels, mice and birds can significantly affect the populations of these animals.

• Many people have responded to the problems created by development. In 1993, the U. S. Department of the Interior resolved to preserve a large piece of Florida wetlands and begin an aggressive restoration project.

• Much can be done to preserve wildlife in our own backyards. Planting native plants, providing food and water stations and leaving some areas undisturbed all help bring back the balance of nature.

The Backyard Wildlife chapter of the *Animal Tracks Activity Guide* corresponds to the Squirrel chapter of the *Animal Tracks* children's book.

1. An Ant's View of Life

Subjects:
Environmental Science, Language Arts, Art

Process Skills:
Exploring, observing, describing, writing, using imagination and visualization

Grades:
3–6

Cognitive Task Level:
Average

Time for Activity:
20 minutes observing,
30 minutes writing

Key Vocabulary:
Imagine, empathy, compassion, effect

Intended Learning Outcomes:
Completing this activity will allow students to:
- Imagine what life would be like if they were ants or another type of animal
- Describe their experiences with writing and art
- Develop greater empathy and compassion for all living things.

Background

Often, we forget or are unaware of the impact our behavior has on others. By "putting ourselves in someone else's shoes," we can gain understanding and compassion. This activity requires students to pretend that they are ants. They crawl or kneel in a grassy area, and describe what things would look like if they were suddenly changed into ants. Then, they use their creativity and imagination to write stories or draw pictures describing their experiences as ants. This can be used as an introduction to discussion about how animals are affected by changes that humans make on their environment. Your students should have a different view on life after their experience.

Materials
- ❑ Clipboards or sketch pads for each student
- ❑ Pencils, crayons or colored pencils
- ❑ Natural area on or near school grounds
- ❑ Magnifying glass (one per student or pair of students)

Procedure

1. Use the ant maze in *Animal Tracks* children's book to introduce your students to the life of ants. Explain that all animals have complex lives. For example, what would it be like to be an ant for a day? To ants, a human being must appear as a giant. A crumb of food would be a feast to bring back to the ant hill. So that they may experience this, tell your students they have suddenly been transformed into ants — tiny black insects that live outdoors. They can bring a magnifying glass. They should also bring paper and pencil to record their experiences and share them with others. Hand them their clipboards, pencils and magnifying glass, and take them to a grassy place outdoors.

2. As ants, they must get as close to the ground as they can, on their hands and knees or crawling. Blades of grass would tower over them. Birds would be frightening predators. As they move, they must describe what they see from an ant's-eye view. They can write their experiences or draw pictures of what they see from their ant's size.

3. After about 10 to 15 minutes, call your students back to class and give them time to finish their stories and drawings, if necessary.

4. Have your students share their stories or pictures with the class. Ask them what effect this activity had on them. Do they view life differently now? Has the activity made them more aware of the effects of humans on animals? Did any of them imagine a huge foot coming down and nearly squashing them? What if they were another sort of animal? Encourage them to conduct this activity on their own, with other types of animals.

Extensions/Modifications

- A simpler version of this activity is to simply take your students out to a natural area and write down or draw pictures of all the animals they can see in a period of time.

- A team of students sets up a boundary, using a yard of string and four sticks. Acting as ants, they experience life in that square. They then draw a map of the square, or give other teams a tour of their "world."

- Have your students expand their stories by selecting another animal and describing how life would be different from their ant experience. For example, how is being an eagle different from being an ant?

- Invite a local zoo or museum representative to come to the class and bring a live animal. After the presenter describes the life of that animal, ask your students to imagine what it would be like to be that animal.

2. Building Bird and Squirrel Feeders

Subjects:
Science, Social Studies, Environmental Studies

Process Skills:
Sequencing, estimating, reading and following directions, forming models, problem solving

Grades:
3–6

Cognitive Task Level:
Simple

Time for Activity:
One class period, or 50 minutes

Key Vocabulary:
Wildlife, environment, care, consideration, recycle

Intended Learning Outcomes:
Completing this activity will allow students to:

- Learn how to make a bird and/or squirrel feeder by reusing milk cartons and other items

- Learn ways to help create a desirable environment for birds and other animals.

Background

Children learn to care for their pets by providing them with what they need to live: food, water and shelter. The can also learn to care for wild animals by helping provide them with what they can use — a backyard or school yard with plenty of vegetation for shelter, a bird bath or water dish for water and a feeding station for food. Creating an inviting environment for wild animals brings them closer to us, allowing us to observe them and learn about them.

Simple bird feeders can be made by spreading peanut butter onto pine cones or toilet paper rolls and rolling them in bird seed. The two feeders described here highlight re-use of items that might otherwise be discarded.

Materials
For the Bird Feeder:
- ❑ Milk cartons or plastic soda bottles
- ❑ 12-inch wooden sticks or dowel rods
- ❑ Wire or string

For the Bird/Squirrel Feeder:
- ❑ Used aluminum pie pan, microwave dish or similar dish
- ❑ A piece of wood slightly larger than the pan
- ❑ One piece of wood for the roof (same length wood as the pan)
- ❑ Two short pieces of wood for the posts
- ❑ 8 nails and 2 short wood screws
- ❑ Hammer and screwdriver
- ❑ 2-pound bag of sunflower or mixed birdseed and 1 small bag for each student

Here is a step-by-step diagram of what to do:

Cut openings on both sides with lots of room at the bottom for seed.

Strong string or wire

1/4" diameter dowel or small stick long enough to go through the carton and have room for a bird to sit on either side.

Here is a step-by-step diagram of what to do:

One nail or screw

Aluminum pie or roasting pan

A board larger than the board under the pan

A board slightly larger than the pan

Two nails or screws

1" x 4" boards 12" tall

Three nails or screws

Procedure

1. Prepare your students for this activity by discussing with them the basic needs of all living things: Food, water, a place to hide from enemies and bad weather and a place to raise a family. Ask them to think of ways to provide food, water and shelter to the wild animals in their backyards or in the school yard. Answers should include ideas like planting plants that provide shelter, installing a bird bath or water dish and making feeding stations for animals.

2. If you are making the bird feeder, tell your students to bring empty milk cartons or 2-liter plastic soda bottles to class. Assist your students in cutting holes in the containers for the birdseed and the dowel. Attach strong wire to the top of the feeder for hanging from a corner of a building or the branch of a tree. *(See diagram.)* Your students can decorate their bird feeders if they want to. Fill with birdseed, and hang.

3. For the squirrel feeder, have them bring in old aluminum pie plates or plastic containers at least 9" in diameter. It is helpful if you pre-drill the screw holes into the wood roof, base and posts to ease construction by the students.

4. Break students into groups to work on the activity. Encourage students to help each other.

5. Either feeder can be hung from a tree branch, left on the ground or placed on a stump or wall. Encourage students to select a site where they already observed birds or squirrels. Have small bags of bird seed ready to give the students when they take their feeders home. Remind students that some areas are safer than others. A feeder on the ground makes birds vulnerable to cats. A feeder in the open away from the safety of brush may makes birds vulnerable to predatory birds, like hawks.

Extensions/Modifications

- If your students are younger, or need more assistance than you can give them, save this activity for parent-teacher night or for another event where parents can help their children conduct the activity.
- For simple bird/squirrel feeders, just roll toilet paper rolls or pine cones in peanut butter, followed by rolling in bird seed. Set these out on the ground or hang from a tree branch with yarn. Or, simply place a dish with seed out in an open area.
- Establish a nature area in your school yard. Place a couple of feeders there and add a water dish or bird bath. Encourage your group to make the feeders and sell them to help raise funds to purchase trees and shrubs that will provide shelter for animals in your nature area. See *An Animal Invitation* in this chapter for ideas on how to create a nature area.

3. What To Do With an Empty Lot?

Subjects:
Science, Math, Social Studies, Economics, Health, Ethics

Process Skills:
Reading and presenting a role, team building, developing and writing strategy, presenting a point of view, decision making

Grades:
4–12

Cognitive Task Level:
Average

Time for Activity:
One or more class periods, depending on how the activity is conducted

Key Vocabulary:
Economics, environment, open space, role play

Intended Learning Outcomes:
Completing this activity will allow students to:
- Act out a role
- Experience the difficulty of making decisions about complex issues
- Observe how one decision can affect the environment, the people, the economy and financial interests of many people.

Background

Open space is a valuable asset to any community. It provides an aesthetic rest for the eye, and often is host to a wide variety of organisms. But land has economic value, and open spaces are disappearing in cities as owners develop their land. Owning and maintaining land is costly; owners must pay a variety of taxes and fees for their land.

Developing the land is one way to generate funds to alleviate the costs of ownership. Selling the land after property values have risen is a common way to make money in our economy. This role-play activity presents a simplified version of what occurs every day, as property owners make decisions about what to do with their land.

In assigning roles to your students, be sure to create diverse groups of students with varied interests. Part of the effectiveness of this activity comes when a person is required to play a role that he or she does not initially like. The result can be greater understanding of divergent sides of an issue. To add emphasis to this approach, you may want to tell the students they will be graded on how well they argue for the issue they have been assigned. Leave time after the role play for a discussion about how the students felt when they presented their cases, and how they felt when the proposal they represented was not selected.

Materials

❑ Pencils and paper for students
❑ Handouts:
 • *Role-play activity sheets*
 • *Map of empty lot*

Procedure

1. Explain the activity to students. The first handout is a map of an open space in town. It is about the size of one football field, and has a natural stream running along one edge of the property. The owner of the lot has been approached by different groups who have expressed interest in using the land.

Using the role-play handouts provided, break your class into interest groups and assign their roles. Depending on how much time you want to use for this lesson, you may want your students to conduct more research on their topics. Or, give them about ten minutes to read their handouts and develop a strategy for their argument. Have them write their points on the handouts so that they have a written strategy to present to the class. Help students write their strategies and answer questions they may have.

Owners: While the rest of the groups are developing their strategies, have the owners do the math questions. Tell them that they must pay attention to all the arguments, and that they must vote at the end of the period on what they plan to do with their land. They will be able to choose only one of the options presented.

Conglomerate Company:
This company has been cited for dumping chemical waste in the past. None of the other groups knows this. Tell the group they can decide whether they want to inform the *Owners* about this or not. If they do not make the announcement themselves, inform them that at some point in the presentation, you (the teacher) will act as "whistle blower" and inform the *Owners* of this fact.

2. After ten minutes, begin the presentations. All other groups must stop talking and listen to the presentations. At the start of each presentation, have the group write its name on the blackboard. Give each group five minutes to present its argument. After the presentation, the students will sit down and the next group will begin.

3. After the presentations have been made, allow the *Owners* a chance to reach a decision. You may want to be with them, or send a teacher's aid to supervise them. Give them five minutes to make their decision. During this time, have each student from the other groups write down what he or she thinks should be done with the land, and whether this differs from the views of the group he or she was in.

4. The *Owners* come back and tell the class what they decided to do and why.

5. Lead a discussion about how the students felt when they presented their cases, and how they felt when their proposal was or was not selected.

Extensions/Modifications

• Have your students attend a city planning meeting, or listen to one if it is broadcast on the radio where you live. Lead a discussion about what they heard and learned. Ask them if they feel differently about land development now than they did before. If they do, ask them why.

• Find a vacant lot in your own town, and use the real life scenario in the class. Have your students write down their recommendations and send them to the land owner or city planning office.

• Invite a city planner to speak to your class. Be sure the planner addresses all the points that are presented in this role play.

Map of Empty Lot

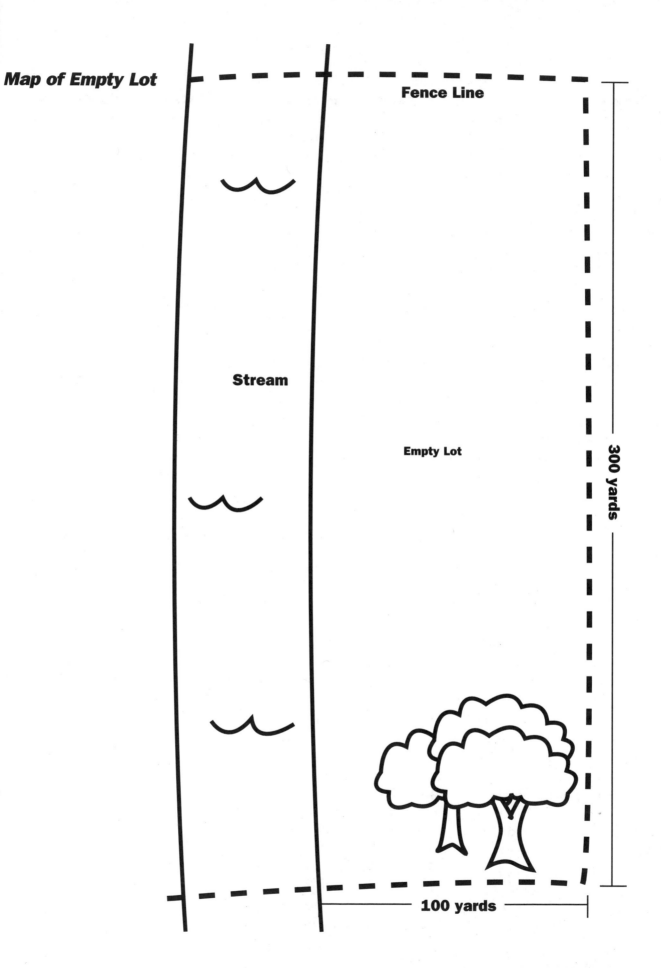

Fence Line

Stream

Empty Lot

300 yards

100 yards

Group 1— Owners

You are the owners of the property. You have been approached by different groups who wish to use your property for their own purposes. You must make a decision about what you want to do with your property.

Presently, your property is an empty lot in the center of town. As owners, you pay property taxes of $250.00 per year. You have owned the property for ten years. You bought the land from the city for $5,000.00 ten years ago. The value of the lot is now worth $10,000.00. Write down the total amount you have paid for this lot on the line below:

$250.00 per year X 10 years = _____

Original purchase price = _____

TOTAL expenditure for lot = _____

Current value of the lot = _____

Since so many people are interested in your lot, you have asked them to attend a meeting where each group will tell you why it wants to use your land. Your group must then make a decision about what to do with the land.

Group 2 — Gardeners' Group

You are members of the local gardening group. You want to use the land so that you can grow fresh vegetables and sell them to earn money. You also want to start a Student Gardening Corps, where students learn gardening skills and help run the garden. You also want to give vegetables to the homeless kitchen so that they can feed homeless people. You are a non-profit organization, but you are willing to pay the owners $250.00 per year to rent the land. This happens to be the same amount that the owners pay in property tax.

What is the name of your organization?

_____

List three reasons why your group should have the lot. These are the reasons you will present to the owners.

1. _____

2. _____

3. _____

How much money are you willing to pay the owners for the lot?

_____

Group 3 — Environmentalists

Your group believes the lot should be left as open space. The lot has been wild for ten years, and is the largest piece of open space in town. It's home to several species of birds, small mammals and insects. The stream has fish, frogs and turtles. The land has some native plants growing on it. You want the lot to remain as it has been for the past ten years. Your group does not have any money to buy the lot, nor do you want to own it. You just believe that the Owners should preserve the lot as open space.

What is the name of your organization?

_____

List three reasons why your group thinks the lot should be left undisturbed. These are the reasons you will present to the owners.

1. _____

2. _____

3. _____

Is your group willing to pay any money for the lot?

_____

Group 4 — Parents Group

You think the lot should be made into a park. The native vegetation should be cleared, and replaced with grass. Playgrounds and picnic tables should be installed. This park would be closer to many people who have to travel a long way to get to another park. Your group asked the city to purchase the land for the park, and the city has said it would buy back the land for the price it was sold for ten years ago: $5,000.00. However, the land is now worth $10,000.00.

What is the name of your organization?

_____

List three reasons why your group should have the lot. These are the reasons you will present to the owners.

1. _____

2. _____

3. _____

How much money are you willing to pay the owners for the lot?

_____

Group 5 — Office Building Developers

You would like to buy the lot and build an office building for your growing company. The building would provide 100 new jobs. Your company is willing to pay the Owners the present property value of $10,000.00 for the lot.

What is the name of your organization?

_____

List three reasons why your group should have the lot. These are the reasons you will present to the owners.

1. _____
2. _____
3. _____

How much money are you willing to pay the owners for the lot?

_____

Group 6 — Conglomerate Company

Your company wants to buy the lot to build a mini-mall. The mall will have a food store, a dry cleaner, a pinball arcade and a photo lab. The mall will create 50 local jobs, so it has an important economic value. However, your company has been cited for environmental violations in the past for dumping chemicals into local creeks. You still dump chemicals secretly and pay the fines when you are caught. Your company has a lot of money, and could make a lot of money on the mall. You offer the owners $20,000.00 for their lot, which is twice the present value of the property.

What is the name of your organization?

_____

List three reasons why your group should have the lot. These are the reasons you will present to the owners.

1. _____
2. _____
3. _____

How much money are you willing to pay the owners for the lot?

_____

4. An Animal Invitation

Subjects:
Science, Language Arts, Social Studies, Environmental Science

Process Skills:
Working cooperatively, estimating costs, forming hypotheses, predicting outcomes, discussing options, making decisions, communicating with others

Grades:
4–12

Cognitive Task Level:
Average to difficult

Time for Activity:
Several class periods, depending on teacher preference

Key Vocabulary:
Drought resistant, enhance, habitat, native

Intended Learning Outcomes:
Completing this activity will allow students to:
- Create an inviting place for wildlife on the school grounds
- Determine what native plants and trees are good food and habitat
- Plan and execute a project within the community
- Enjoy the benefits of providing food and shelter for local wildlife.

Background

All living things have the same basic needs: food, water and shelter. Urban areas can be full of wildlife, but there must be enough places for them to satisfy their basic needs. This activity requires students to learn about local animals, find out how their basic needs can be met and pursue ways to satisfy those needs on the school grounds.

One of the greatest benefits of this activity is developing an appreciation for the value of natural animal habitats to all living things. By adding flowering plants and trees, and food and water stations, both animals and people benefit from an improved environment. Because you are planting food for wildlife to eat and habitat to live in, it's especially important to seek out safe, organic gardening methods for your wildlife habitat.

Materials

Before you buy materials, try to get them donated by a local gardening group, nature organization, parks and recreation department or local business.
- ❏ Mulch
- ❏ Plants
- ❏ Shovels
- ❏ Organic fertilizer or compost
- ❏ Watering container or hose
- ❏ Books on local plants and animals, organic gardening and feeding stations
- ❏ Handout:
  - *Sample press release*

Procedure

There are a variety of steps that need to be completed in order to achieve success. As teacher, you can decide how many tasks you will do yourself, and how many of them you would like your students to do.

1. Locate a site. Take a walk through the school grounds. Identify spots where plants could be planted or bird feeders placed. Try to pick spots that are easy to see from your classroom so that you can enjoy the fruits of the project all day long. Even a site as small as one square yard is big enough for shrubs and flowers.

2. Check with the school principal and custodial staff before you start. You may not be aware of concerns that would have a negative impact on your project. Assure them that your project will not invite undesirable creatures, like house rats and cockroaches. These animals usually thrive on highly disturbed, human impacted areas. They are not usually attracted to wild habitat.

3. Conduct research. Find out what native plants occur in your area. Bookstores and libraries are full of books on organic gardening and creating natural habitats.

4. Decide what animals you want to attract. Find out what animals already visit the area. If you live in a highly urbanized area, it may not be realistic to create a garden to attract deer. But you can create a garden that supports seed-eating birds (such as sparrows or finches), insect-eating birds (such as robins) or butterflies. You may also decide to add colorful flowers merely to brighten the natural habitat. Create a blueprint of the habitat that uses the resources to their fullest. Contact the National Wildlife Federation's Backyard Wildlife Habitat Program, and request materials to aid your preparation.

5. Determine stewardship responsibilities. Once your class has made a commitment to invite wild animals into the neighborhood, you must fulfill that responsibility by keeping the plants alive and lush, and refilling food and water stations, even in winter and summer. Birds, in particular, can come to depend on feeding stations during the winter months when wild food is scarce.

6. Get the supplies you need to start. Find ways to raise the money to acquire the trees, shrubs or plants. Sell bird and squirrel feeders (see Building Bird and Squirrel Feeders in this chapter), or use another fund-raiser. Contact state government agencies that manage natural resources, game or fish. They may provide free trees and shrubs. Students can also seek help from the business community, local adult organizations, the school board, mayor or city council.

7. After your preparations are complete, you can start digging! Schedule a planting day. Be sure to take photographs before and after you complete the project. Invite other members of the neighborhood to come and help. Have your stu-

dents distribute flyers or put an ad in the local newspaper to encourage extra assistance. See the Sample Press Release for ideas.

8. Make working on the natural habitat a part of your regular curriculum. Even a few minutes two or three times a week spent working on your natural habitat can make a big difference, both in the health of the habitat and in the attitudes of your students.

9. After the new habitat is completed, be certain your class observes what insects, animals and birds have been attracted to the habitat area. Take notes about the type of animals, what they appear to be eating and where they appear to be living. Students should be encouraged to submit updated stories to their school and local newspapers about the results.

Modifications/Extensions

- To generate interest within the class, invite a representative from the state Game and Fish Commission or state Department of Natural Resources to speak about neighborhood wildlife and to help evaluate the space. They may also provide trees, shrubs and seeds for the project.
- Invite a representative from a local National Audubon Society or Wilderness Society chapter to talk about any specific conditions in the community that relate to or may impact wildlife.

- Consider the following specialized natural habitat garden themes.

Herb Garden: Many native herbs occur throughout the United States, and have attractive flowers and bloom for extended periods. They also can provide an opportunity for more activities — like learning about their medicinal or culinary uses.

Butterfly Garden: Find out what flowers and shrubs are most attractive to butterflies. Other nectar-loving animals will be attracted as well. You can also make a hummingbird garden if you use plants that are irresistible to hummingbirds and hang hummingbird feeders.

Seed-Eaters Garden: Plant native plants that re-seed themselves every year. They also provide excellent food for seed-eating birds and small mammals.

Native Fruit Trees: Planting fruit trees will encourage squirrels, opossums, raccoons and birds.

Sample Press Release

School Name _____

School Address _____

(or use school letterhead)

For Immediate Release

The students of (name of school) are creating a natural habitat area at school. We will be planting plants to encourage local wildlife, creating feeding and water stations and becoming caretakers of the habitat.

We seek donations of plants, soil, mulch and gardening tools, as well as interested people who can help us on planting day, (date of planting day).

(You can also include details on the goals and intended results of the project; quotes from teachers, administrators and/or students about why the project is important; and its accessibility by the public.)

For more information or to make donations, please call (teacher's name) at XXX-XXX-XXXX.

Resources for Backyard Wildlife

Field Guides

- *National Audubon Society North American Bird Feeder Handbook,* by Robert Burton. Dorling Kindersly Press. This combines the best of field guide and natural history handbook. Beautiful color photos show examples of the most common backyard birds.
- *Peterson First Guides.* Houghton Mifflin Company. This series is excellent for both children and adults.

Books for Adults

- *Sharing Nature with Children,* by Joseph Bharat Cornell. Ananda Publications. This was one of the first books on developing outdoor awareness in children, and is still one of the best.
- *Uncommon Fruits Worthy of Attention: A Gardener's Guide,* by Lee Reich. Addison-Wesley Publishing Company, Inc. Includes good information about native fruit-bearing trees, as well as where and how to plant them.
- *The Natural Habitat Garden,* by Ken Druse. Clarkson Potter Publishers. A beautiful picture book of native plant gardens.

Books for Students

- *A Gift of A Tree,* by Greg Henry Quinn. Scholastic books, Inc. An excellent book that discusses the many functions of trees and backyard habitats. This book comes with a tree-starter seed kit.
- *Bugs,* by Nancy Winslow Parker and Joan Richards Wright. Mulberry Paperback Books. A very nice handbook with illustrations of common insects. Poems start each section.
- *My First Garden Book: A Life-Size Guide to Growing Things at Home,* by Angela Wilkes. Alfred A. Knopf Co. Beautifully photographed, this book offers many simple gardening activities as well as plenty of information about gardening.
- *The Complete Birdhouse Book,* by Donald and Lillian Stokes. Little, Brown and Company. This guide contains excellent instructions on how to build birdhouses, as well as information about the birds who use them. Perfect for home or class projects.

Organizations

- *National Wildlife Federation,* Backyard Wildlife Habitat Program, 8925 Leesburg Pike, Vienna, VA 22184; Phone: 703-790-4438.

Household Chemicals

The Challenge

Some chemical products used in and around our homes and schools are harmful to our health and environment. They can enter the air, water and soil, and cause problems for humans and other animals. By becoming educated about what materials are toxic, and finding safe, effective alternatives, we can reduce our exposure to toxic chemicals and reduce their effect on the environment.

Did You Know?

- The average home contains more chemicals today than the average chemical laboratory did 100 years ago.
- Toxic chemicals dumped in landfills can leach into the groundwater. Chemicals sent to incinerators can end up in the air. Those flushed down the drain can end up in rivers and lakes, threatening plants and animals there.

- More than 21 million tons of soap and laundry detergent are used in the United States. Phosphate, a chemical used in some detergents, creates serious problems for the environment. Detergent companies are now removing phosphates from their products.
- Americans use nearly one billion gallons of motor oil each year. 350 million gallons of it are dumped into the environment. As little as one quart of motor oil contaminates 250,000 gallons of drinking water.
- Many non-toxic products clean just as well as their toxic counterparts, and cost less to buy. The acid in lemon juice is so strong it can clean aluminum. The broth from a boiled potato can remove some grease stains from clothing.

The Household Chemicals chapter of the *Animal Tracks Activity Guide* corresponds to the Rabbit chapter of the *Animal Tracks* children's book.

1. Words of Warning

Subjects:
Science, Environmental Science, Language Arts, Health

Process Skills:
Reading, writing, deciphering clues, organizing information, developing vocabulary

Grades:
4–8

Cognitive Task Level:
Average to difficult

Time for Activity:
20 to 30 minutes

Intended Learning Outcomes:
Completing this activity will allow students to:
- Learn the definitions of words associated with toxics
- Develop vocabulary skills about an important environmental issue
- Gain a greater understanding for the different levels of health concern associated with household chemicals.

Background
Today, more and more of our household products contain complex chemicals that are hazardous, or become hazardous when mixed with other products. These include such common items as chlorine bleach, nail polish, carpet cleaner, oven cleaner and used motor oil. These materials end up in our garbage cans and are then buried in our landfills or flushed into our sewage system. Health problems can result when even small quantities of these chemicals leak into the groundwater and into our drinking water.

This activity gives students an opportunity to develop their vocabulary and learn to spell and pronounce words that could affect their health and safety. It serves as an introduction to the other activities, because it provides valuable vocabulary meanings to words that students will be encountering in the other lessons. In particular, you can discuss with your students the different levels of toxicity and how they are identified by the words *warning, caution* and *danger.* This will help your students know what level of concern to have about different household products.

Materials
❑ Handouts:
  - *Word Search*
  - *Glossary*
  - *Fill-In Worksheet*

Procedure
1. Before you hand out the word search worksheet, you may choose to put the words on the board and review their meanings with your students. Ask students which words they already know. Have them guess at the meanings of some of the other words.

2. Hand out the word search and fill-in worksheets and the glossary. You may conduct this either as an in-class assignment or as a homework assignment. Depending on the class level, your students may need additional help with some of the words.

Extensions/Modifications
- You may elect to use only one portion of this activity to start the unit on household chemicals, and save the other portion as a follow-up.
- The *Words of Warning Fill-in Worksheet* can be used as a test for the unit.
- If you have ESL (English as a Second Language) students in your class, be sure they understand the meanings of the words in their own language.
- Invite a local hazardous waste specialist from the community to come to the class and explain his or her job and responsibilities.

Words of Warning Word Search

Name _____

```
B P S O L V E N T A S R D U
X I N G E S T W O E T T A P
S R O B V C F E R D O X N Q
T O E D N K H Y R Z X M G T
Y G E G E X P L O S I V E X
V R V Z M G O T S U C X R P
R E U S E X R X P O I S O N
T W Y S H K X A B D W L R L
F C A U T I O N D R Y Q M E
H H J S T E U N P A W Y G T
E E X F L A M M A B L E H
A M D W N J L X M R F L O A
L I R W A R N I N G H B E L
T C X G L G S N P Y T W X D
H A Z A R D O U S L Y Z B O
X L M Y T W L J G F D S W S
W S C O R R O S I V E R P E
```

Words:

Explosive	Toxic	Health
Warning	Caution	Ingest
Lethal Dose	Hazardous	Chemical
Corrosive	Poison	Solvent
Danger	Reuse	
Flammable	Biodegradable	

Words of Warning Fill-In Worksheet

Name _____

Below are incomplete sentences. Find the words in the Words of Warning Glossary that answer the sentences correctly. Then find the words hidden in the Word Search.

1. To _____ something means to swallow it.

2. Materials that are consumed by microscopic organisms and decomposed are

    _____

3. A _____ is a substance that can cause harm when we inhale, eat or absorb it.

4. A _____ is another name for something that causes harm when we ingest it.

5. _____ waste is something that is thrown away and that is harmful to living things or the environment.

6. The _____ is the amount of a substance that causes death.

7. When something catches fire easily, it is _____.

8. A _____ is a complex substance that is man-made.

9. Something that blows up is called an _____.

10. _____
    substances burn the skin and eyes.

11. When seen on a product package, this word means it contains a slightly toxic substance with a lethal dose for humans of one ounce or more: _____.

12. When the word "_____" appears on a package, it contains a moderately toxic substance that has a lethal dose to humans of one teaspoon to one ounce of the substance. Handle this product very carefully.

13. A product that is labeled with the word _____ is very toxic and has a lethal dose for humans of a few drops to a teaspoon. You should never touch a substance like this.

14. The reason we learn about household chemicals is to stay in good _____.

15. It is possible to _____ some of our household products so that we do not have to dispose of them in the garbage can after only one use.

16. A _____ is a liquid that dissolves solids. Water is the most common one.

Words of Warning Glossary

Biodegradable — A material that is consumed by microscopic organisms and decomposed.

Caution — When seen on a product package, this word means it contains a slightly toxic substance.

Chemical — Complex substance, usually man-made.

Corrosive — A substance that burns eyes and skin. A strong corrosive can eat away other substances like metal or skin.

Danger — When seen on a product package, this word means it contains a very toxic substance that can be deadly when ingested, even in small amounts.

Explosive — A substance that blows up and makes a loud noise under certain conditions.

Flammable — Easily set on fire.

Hazardous Wastes — Substances that are thrown away and are dangerous to living things.

Health — Of body and mind.

Ingest — To swallow or eat.

Lethal dose — The amount of a toxic that causes death. The lethal dose varies depending on the age and size of the individual who ingests it.

Poison — A substance that causes harm when we inhale, eat or absorb it through our skin.

Reuse — To use again. This saves landfill space and reduces garbage problems.

Solvents — Liquids that dissolve solids. Water is the most common non-toxic solvent that we use. An example is salt dissolving in water.

Toxic — Poisonous; having the effect of a poison. (See *poison*.)

Warning — When seen on a product package, this word means it contains a moderately toxic substance.

Words of Warning Fill-In Worksheet

Teacher's Version

Below are incomplete sentences. Find the words in the *Words of Warning Glossary* that answer the sentences correctly. Then find the words hidden in the *Word Search.*

1. To <u>ingest</u> something means to swallow it.

2. Materials that are consumed by microscopic organisms and decomposed are <u>biodegradable.</u>

3. A <u>poison</u> is a substance that can cause harm when we inhale, eat or absorb it.

4. A <u>toxic</u> is another name for something that causes harm when we ingest it.

5. <u>Hazardous</u> waste is something that is thrown away and that is harmful to living things or the environment.

6. The <u>lethal dose</u> is the amount of a substance that causes death.

7. When something catches fire easily, it is <u>flammable.</u>

8. A <u>chemical</u> is a complex substance that is man-made.

9. Something that blows up is called an <u>explosive.</u>

10. <u>Corrosive</u> substances burn the skin and eyes.

11. When seen on a product package, this word means it contains a slightly toxic substance with a lethal dose for humans of one ounce or more: <u>Caution.</u>

12. When the word "<u>warning</u>" appears on a package, it contains a moderately toxic substance that has a lethal dose to humans of one teaspoon to one ounce of the substance. Handle this product very carefully.

13. A product that is labeled with the word <u>danger</u> is very toxic and has a lethal dose for humans of a few drops to a teaspoon. You should never touch a substance like this.

14. The reason we learn about household chemicals is to stay in good <u>health.</u>

15. It is possible to <u>reuse</u> some of our household products so that we do not have to dispose of them in the garbage can after only one use.

16. A <u>solvent</u> is a liquid that dissolves solids. Water is the most common one.

Words of Warning Word Search

(Teacher's version)

```
B X S O L V E N T X X X D X
X I N G E S T X X X T X A X
X X O X X X X X X X O X N X
X X X D X X X X X X X X G X
X X X X E X P L O S I V E X
X X X X X G X X X C X R X
R E U S E X R X P O I S O N
X X X X X X X A X X X X X L
X C A U T I O N D X X X X E
H H X X X X X X X A X X X T
E E X X F L A M M A B L E H
A M X X X X X X X X X L X A
L I X W A R N I N G X X E L
T C X X X X X X X X X X X D
H A Z A R D O U S X X X X O
X L X X X X X X X X X X X S
X S C O R R O S I V E X X E
```

Words:
Explosive
Warning
Lethal Dose
Corrosive
Danger
Flammable
Toxic
Caution
Hazardous
Poison
Reuse
Biodegradable
Health
Ingest
Chemical
Solvent

2. What Does the Label Say?

Subjects:
Science, Environmental Science, Language Arts

Process Skills:
Reading, writing, deciphering clues, developing vocabulary

Grades:
3–6

Cognitive Task Level:
Average to difficult

Time for Activity:
20 minutes

Key Vocabulary:
Warning, caution, danger, poison, toxic

Intended Learning Outcomes:
Completing this activity will allow students to:
• Learn to read the labels of household products
• Develop vocabulary skills
• Gain a greater understanding for the different levels of health concern associated with household chemicals.

Background

Most people never look at the labels on their favorite household products. However, all products that are potentially hazardous require a warning label. Learning to read the label can reveal a great deal of information. The label explains the level of caution that should be maintained during use. For instance, some products simply say, "Avoid contact with eyes, flush thoroughly with water." Others say, "Extremely dangerous if swallowed, keep out of reach of children." By learning how to read the label, students can begin to understand what should be considered a genuine health concern, and what requires intelligent caution when used properly.

Use the *Words Of Warning Glossary* provided in the *Words of Warning* activity to help you determine the meanings of the words found on the warning labels of packages. You may wish to use this activity to prepare your students for the Household Chemicals Home Survey. Be sure to find out the telephone number of the poison control hotline in your area.

Materials

❑ Common household product packages that contain warning labels, such as jewelry cleaner, household cleaners, nail polish remover, medication, etc. If possible, photocopy the package warnings and make overhead transparencies to show your students.

❑ Handout:
  • *How to Read A Label*

Procedure

1. Show your students examples of common household products that contain warning labels.

2. Explain the meanings of the words to the students, using the Words of Warning Glossary.

3. Divide the students into groups of four or five. Give three different product packages to each group, or give them photocopies of the labels. Have them look for the six different items on the Labels Checklist, and fill out the answers for each item.

4. Use this activity to spark a discussion about hazardous household chemicals. Address students' concerns about accidental overuse or incorrect use. Get the poison control hotline number for your neighborhood and make it available to your students.

Extensions/Modifications

• This activity can be conducted as a demonstration for younger children.
• You may choose to expand this activity by having your students write to the manufacturer of a particular product, and request additional information about the product.
• Teach students the proper procedures for a chemical or poison emergency. Find the poison hotline telephone number in the front pages of your telephone book. Or, invite a local health official to teach students how to handle an emergency.

How To Read A Label

*Name:*_____

Household products that contain hazardous substances are required to carry warnings that inform people of the risks involved. The label should contain the following information listed below:

1. The brand and the common and/or chemical name. "Bleach" is a common name, while "sodium hypochlorite" is the chemical name for this common household product.

2. The product description or some clue about what it's meant to do. Laundry soap and paint remover are examples.

3. Words of warning.
- "Caution" is used for mildly toxic substances
- "Warning" is used on moderately toxic substances
- "Danger" is used on highly toxic, flammable, or corrosive substances
- "Poison" is used on all toxic substances

4. Instructions for safe use and any precautions. "Keep out of reach of children," or "Use in well-ventilated area" are examples.

5. First-aid instructions in case the produce is misused or ingested. "Induce vomiting" is one example. Remember to call the Poison Hotline or 911 in an emergency.

6. Name, address and phone number of the manufacturer. If you would like more information about the product, call or write to the company.

Look at the label of a product and try to find all six categories. Write the answer in the space provided. Use the guide above to remember what each category means.

1 Brand and common or chemical names	2 Product description	3 Warning words	4 Safety precautions	5 First aid instructions	6 Manufacturer's name, address or telephone number
Chlorine bleach, sodium hypochlorite	*Bleach*	*Danger: Corrosive — can burn skin*	*Keep out of reach of children*	*If in eyes, rinse with plenty of water for at least 15 minutes*	*The Chemical Company, Anytown, USA*

ENVIRONMENTALLY
SOUND

ALL PURPOSE CLEANER

All Purpose Cleaner removes grease, grime and stains quickly and easily from most surfaces.

How to use: For use on appliances, walls, floors sealed wood, stone, or any other washable surface. As with other cleaners, it is recommended that a small area be tested before applying. Use full strength. Leaves no residue. No rinsing necessary.

Contents: Cleaning agent derived from fermented corn and coconuts, Organic Surfactant, Vinegar, Citrus Oils.

Caution: Avoid contact with eyes. In case of eye contact, flush with water. Do not take internally. Keep out of reach of children.

- **Environmentally Sound**
- **Biodegradable**
- **All replenishable resource product**
- **Non-toxic**

- **Non-abrasive**
- **Preservative free**
- **Phosphate free**
- **No Petroleum or petroleum by-products**

* All ingredients in this product rapidly break down into harmless natural elements.

This product was not tested on animals and contains no animal by-products.

Lotion for dry skin. Rich in special skin-softening emollients.

The luxurious body-cleansing bath and shower gelee created especially for dry skin that is sensitive to wind and weather. The formula is moisture-rich, containing Vitamin E to smooth, soften, protect, and to help maintain healthy-looking skin. The fragrance surrounds you in a beautiful aura of jasmine, woods and mosses. The effect is fresh and lively. Discover the skin-beautifying and moisturizing benefits of this lotion—the ultimate dimension in bathing.

In the bath: Pour one capful of lotion into the tub and run water vigorously.

In the shower: Squeeze lotion onto your washcloth or sponge, instead of soap.

Caution: As with other similar products, if the lotion gets into eyes, wash thoroughly with water. For adult use only. Keep out of the reach of children.

Pain Reliever for Sinuses

Product Benefits:

Maximum allowable levels of non-aspirin pain reliever and nasal decongestant provide temporary relief of sinus headache pain, pressure and nasal congestion due to colds and flu or hay fever and other allergies.

Contains no ingredients which may cause drowsiness.

DIRECTIONS: Adults and children 12 years and over, 2 tablets every 6 hours, not to exceed 8 tablets in a 24-hour period. Not recommended for children under 12 years of age.
EACH COATED TABLET CONTAINS: acetaminophen 500 mg and pseudoephedrine hydrochloride 30 mg. Also contains: carnauba wax, crospovidone, FD&C Yellow No. 6 Lake, hydroxypropyl methylcellulose, magnesium stearate, microcrystalline cellulose, polyethylene glycol, polysorbate 80, providone, pregelatinized corn starch, stearic acid, and titanium dioxide.
WARNINGS: Do not exceed recommended dosage because at higher doses nervousness, dizziness or sleeplessness may occur. Do not take this product for more than 10 days. If symptoms do not improve or are accompanied by fever that lasts for more than 3 days, or if new symptoms occur, consult a physician. Do not take this product if you have high blood pressure, heart disease, diabetes, thyroid disease, or difficulty in urination due to enlargement of the prostate gland except under the advice and supervision of a physician. As with any drug, if you are pregnant or nursing a baby, seek the advice of a health professional before using this product.
Drug Interaction Precaution: Do not take this product if you are presently taking a prescription antihypertensive or antidepressant drug conatining a monoamine oxidase inhibitor except under the advice and supervision of a physician.
KEEP THIS AND ALL DRUGS OUT OT THE REACH OF CHILDREN. In case of accidental overdose, seek professional assistance or contact a Poison Control Center immediately. Prompt medical attention is critical for adults as well as children even if you do not notice any signs or symptoms.
Store at 15° to 25°C (59° to 77°F) in a dry place and protect from light.

3. Household Chemicals: A Home Survey

Subjects:
Science, Environmental Science, Health

Process Skills:
Organizing, recording data, reading labels

Grades:
3-6

Cognitive Task Level:
Average to difficult

Time for Activity:
30 minutes of homework, 15 minutes in class

Key Vocabulary:
Caution, corrosive, danger, explosive, flammable, poison, warning

Intended Learning Outcomes:
Completing this activity will allow students to:
- Learn about some of the toxic chemicals commonly used in housecleaning supplies
- Conduct a survey of hazardous household products found in their homes, under the supervision of an adult.

Background

Most people do not realize that their homes are filled with toxic chemicals. Most of these products are not dangerous if used properly. But incorrect disposal of household chemicals can result in serious problems. When containers full of chemicals are placed together in a trash can, the containers can break and the chemicals can mix.

It is important to know about proper handling and disposal of household chemicals. To make this activity useful to your students, find out information about local household hazardous waste collection programs. Have your students conduct this Home Survey, and help them inform their parents of the correct disposal of these materials.

Materials
- ❑ Handout:
  - *Where Are The Toxic Products In My Home?*
- ❑ Written information about the proper disposal of household chemicals in your community

Procedure
1. Use the previous activities to prepare your students for this activity.

2. Discuss the various rooms in the house where hazardous chemicals accumulate. Where are they most likely to find household chemicals? The laundry room, bathroom and garage are the most common places to find them. Suggest that they conduct their survey with a parent or other adult.

3. Discuss the results of the survey the next day. What rooms of the house contained the most household chemicals?

4. Have your students describe some of the products they found. Were they surprised at what they found? Do they think they need all those products, or could some of them be replaced with non-toxic alternatives?

5. Discuss with your students how to properly store these toxic products. Are they in the safest place in the house, garage or workshop?

6. Discuss how to dispose of toxic products they no longer need. Simply dumping materials in the garbage can is not usually the best method, as it can create even greater toxic risks. Hand out the information about proper disposal of household chemicals in your community.

Extensions/Modifications
- Take a field trip to the nearby household hazardous waste collection facility.
- Invite a speaker from the household hazardous waste program to speak to the class.

Where Are The Toxic Products In My Home?

Name _____

Toxic household products tend to appear in some rooms more than others. With an adult, conduct a survey of your home. Look in every room for household products that have labels with warning words, such as **caution, toxic, danger** or **warning.**

Using the list of rooms below, indicate how many toxic household products you found. If you can, be specific about the type of product you found. For example, the container may contain medicine, cleaning supplies, solvents or paint.

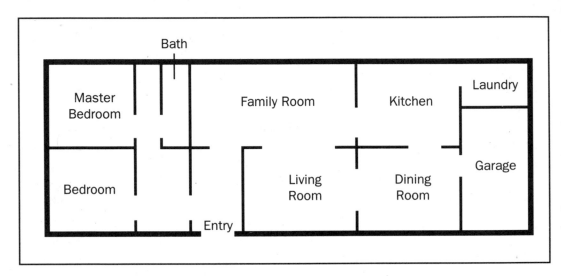

Kitchen _____

Family room _____

Living room _____

Your bedroom _____

Parent's bedroom _____

Bathroom _____

Garage _____

Laundry room _____

What rooms have the highest number of toxic household products? _____

_____

4. On the Spot

Background

Many household cleaning products are based upon some old, well-known non-toxic materials that have been used for centuries. People cleaned their homes, washed their clothes and rid themselves of pests and odors even before synthetic-based cleaners were formulated.

One reason old-fashioned cleaners are regaining popularity is because some people have developed allergies or sensitivities to synthetic cleaners on the market. Most natural cleaners do not cause the same types of allergic reactions or sensitivity as the synthetic ones.

In this activity, students will make hypotheses about which product they think will work best for the job, and then test their hypotheses with experiments. Remember, even some natural products have powerful properties! Warn your students not to touch their eyes, and to wash their hands thoroughly with soap after they finish their experiments. This activity works well in coordination with other activities in this unit, particularly after completing the *Words of Warning* and *What Does the Label Say?* activities.

Materials

Store-bought cleaning supplies:

- ❏ Window cleaner
- ❏ Furniture polish
- ❏ Copper cleaner
- ❏ Stain remover
- ❏ Clear shoe polish or leather cleaner

Alternative cleaning supplies:

- ❏ 2 bottles white vinegar
- ❏ 3 lemons
- ❏ 2 boxes baking soda
- ❏ 1 large bottle olive oil
- ❏ 1 pint milk
- ❏ 1 tube whitening toothpaste

Equipment:

- ❏ 6 clean 100-percent cotton rags
- ❏ 6 teaspoons (tsp.) and 6 table-spoons (Tbs.)
- ❏ 36 cups or dishes for mixing homemade solutions (6 per table)
- ❏ Ruber gloves (optional)
- ❏ Safety glasses (optional)

Items to clean:

- ❏ 6 copper pennies
- ❏ 6 small blocks of wood
- ❏ 6 small swatches of leather
- ❏ Cloths stained with felt pens or ball point pens
- ❏ Cloths stained with crayons
- ❏ Dirty window, piece of glass or mirror (the dirtier the better)
- ❏ Handouts:
  - *Which Works Better?*
  - *Nature's Cleaners*

Procedure

1. To prepare, have your students cut or tear the cotton rags into small (3-inch x 3-inch) pieces. Each group will need about six pieces of rag.

2. Divide the class into six groups, and have them work together at a table or work station. Explain the purpose of the activity and distribute the materials. Hint: this activity may go more smoothly if you have students help you set up the work stations during recess before the activity. WARNING: Be sure the work stations are well supervised by an adult, since the students will handle toxic substances.

3. Have the students follow the instructions, as outlined on the *Which Works Better?* handout. Before they begin, ask them to determine which compound they believe will work better at cleaning. Be sure they explain this hypothesis before they conduct the experiment.

4. After the activity, go through the data sheets together and ask your students which products worked better and why. Answers will vary depending on the products used. Ask your students if they would be willing to change their store-bought products for homemade ones. If they say no, you can use this as a start of a discussion about why synthetic products are so popular. They often do the job faster and with less work. In the case of glass cleaner, which usually does not work any better than vinegar and water, ask your students if they would switch. Why or why not?

Extensions/Modifications

- To simplify this activity, you can conduct it as a demonstration for small groups of students.
- Encourage your students to continue their experiments in the home. Using the *Nature's Cleaners* handout, encourage your students to make up some recipes of their own and try them out. Offer extra credit for students who conduct further experiments and write down their own cleaning recipes.
- Have the students concoct one of the natural alternatives, and prepare it as a take-home gift for a parent.

Resources for Household Chemicals

Books for Adults

- *Clean & Green: The Complete Guide to Nontoxic and Environmentally Safe Housekeeping*, by Annie Berthold-Bond. Ceres Press, 1990.
- *Nontoxic and Natural: A Guide For Consumers; How To Avoid Dangerous Everyday Products and Buy or Make Safe Ones*, by Jeremy P. Tarcher. 1984.
- *Hazardous Waste From Homes*, by John Lord. Enterprise For Education, 1988.
- *How To Clean Everything*, by Alma Chestnut Moore. Simon & Schuster, 1977.

Education Materials for Teachers

- *Green-Keeping Newsletter*, Box 110, Annandale, NY 12504.
- *Toxics In My home? You Bet!* Local Government Commission, Inc., 909 12th Street, Suite 205, Sacramento, CA 95814; 916-448-1198.
- *SLEUTH. Metro Toxicant Program*, Washington State Office of Environmental Education, 17011 Meridien Avenue, N Room 16, Seattle, WA 98133.

For Students

- *The Haz-Kid Report: Household Hazardous Waste* (video). San Bernardino (Ca.) Dept. of Health Services, 1987.
- *50 Simple Things Kids Can Do To Save The Earth*. The Earthworks Press, 1990.

Which Works Better?

Name _____

Conduct the following experiments to find out which product works better at the job it is used for: The store-bought version, or the home-made version.

Product	Store-Bought version (Brand name of product)	Alternative	Hypothesis (Which do you think will work better?)	Results (Explain which worked better and why you think so)
Glass cleaner		Equal parts vinegar and water		
Furniture polish		1 tsp. olive oil + 1 tsp. lemon + 1 tsp. water		
Copper cleaner		2 Tbs. salt + 1 Tbs. vinegar		
Leather polish		1/4 cup olive oil + a few drops lemon juice		
Ink spot removal		2 options: Soak in lemon juice or soak in milk. Rub stain gently. (Try both options.)		
Crayon stain-remover (for clothing)		Make a paste with baking soda and olive oil. Rub gently.		

Nature's Cleaners

Abrasives — An abrasive removes dirt from a surface by scrubbing it off. Nature's abrasives include salt and baking soda. Combining abrasives with acids, like vinegar, creates a very powerful cleanser.

Acids — Acids react chemically with dirt and lift the dirt off a surface. Natural acids include lemon juice, vinegar and ammonia. Like all acids, use these products with care and avoid touching the eyes after use. Even natural acids can be harmful or painful if used without caution.

Pastes — Pastes are alkali, the opposite of an acid. Alkali pastes remove dirt chemically, by bonding with acidic dirt. Applying paste with a soft cloth and allowing it to sit for awhile is very effective. Common alkali pastes include those containing baking soda.

Make your own products!

Using the list below, try making products of your own, and try them in your home. All of these materials are available in the grocery store.

Alum — Cleans stains such as rust on porcelain and removes hard water spots. Very effective when mixed with vinegar or lemon juice.

Baking soda — A mild abrasive, baking soda also absorbs odors and deodorizes.

Borax — A natural mineral mined from the earth, Borax deodorizes and inhibits mold growth.

Chalk — A mild abrasive cleaner that also whitens.

Cream of Tartar — Cleans porcelain, drains and metal.

Pumice — An abrasive, pumice can be used on tough stains.

Salt — A mild abrasive that also inhibits bacteria.

Citrus — Natural acid solvent and cleaner. Removes mineral build-up, tarnish and grease. Also an excellent air freshener.

White vinegar — Cuts grease, removes mineral build-up and inhibits mold growth. Also freshens the air.

Water Conservation

The Water Conservation chapter of the *Animal Tracks Activity Guide* corresponds to the Otter chapter of the *Animal Tracks* children's book.

The Challenge

The more humans there are, the more water we need. That kind of demand, as well as climate changes, can lead to droughts throughout the world. Water shortages also threaten our health and environment.

We think water will always appear when we turn on the tap. We rarely worry about it, except during a flood or drought. Droughts are common, and we can't always predict when they will arrive or how long they'll last.

Half of all Americans get their drinking water from groundwater, which is water that fills the cracks and pores below the surface of the earth.

Fill a glass with water. If that's all the water in the United States, farmers will use two-thirds of it. It takes more than 50 gallons to make eight ounces of milk, 115 gallons to grow the wheat to make one loaf of bread and 40 gallons to help a chicken produce one egg.

Did You Know?

• Water covers 70 percent of the earth's surface. Most of it is salt water in oceans.

• The water we have on earth today is all we will ever have. We can't make "new" water; we're just reusing what's already here.

• Water is the only substance that occurs as a liquid, a gas and a solid in nature.

• Only 3 percent of all the water on earth is fresh. More than two-thirds of that 3 percent is frozen at the north and south poles. All of us share less than 1 percent of all the water on earth.

• We need water to produce lots of the goods we use. It takes from 7 to 25 gallons of water to produce one gallon of gasoline, and it takes 280 gallons of water to produce one Sunday newspaper.

• Half of all Americans get their drinking water from groundwater, which is water that fills the cracks and pores just below the surface of the earth.

1. The Water Cycle

Subjects:

Science, Language Arts, Environmental Studies

Process Skills:

Following directions, observing scientific phenomena, building vocabulary

Grades:

3–6

Cognitive Task Level:

Average to difficult

Time for Activity:

20 to 30 minutes

Key Vocabulary:

Accumulation, condensation, evaporation, gaseous, hydrologic cycle, precipitation, steam, vapor

Intended Learning Outcomes:

Completing this activity will allow students to:

• Learn the four steps in the hydrologic cycle and the three physical states of water

• Observe and describe how water changes as it moves through the hydrologic cycle

• Develop and use new vocabulary words.

Background

Water is one of the most important resources on earth. Water seems magical because it changes its form and is found in all three states of existence. In its liquid state, it is called water, as we know it. In its solid state, water is known as ice. In its gaseous state, water is called steam or vapor.

Water maintains its liquid state between 32° F and 212° F (0 - 100° C). Below 32°, water freezes into ice. Above 212°, water evaporates into steam. Water is stored in all three forms on earth — as ice in glaciers at the North and South polar caps; in its liquid state in our oceans, rivers, lakes and streams; and in its gaseous state as vapor in the air we breathe. You can feel water vapor in the air on a hot and humid day. You can see water vapor condense against a cold glass of milk.

Water is recycled again and again in the hydrologic cycle. Water accumulates, or gathers, in lakes and oceans. On a hot day, the water reaches its vapor point and evaporates into the air. This gas travels upward until it reaches a cold thermal layer above the earth. This thermal layer is so cold that water forms ice crystals. The coldness of the ice causes the warm gaseous water to cool and become liquid. This process is called condensation. Clouds are the result of condensation. As more water vapor condenses at the cold thermal layer, the water particles become large and heavy. These water molecules eventually fall out of the sky as rain. This is called precipitation.

Materials

(For a class of 30 students)

- ❑ 6 portable electric burners
- ❑ 6 aluminum pie plates
- ❑ 5 pounds ice
- ❑ 6 pots or beakers in which to boil water
- ❑ Handouts:
  - *The Hydrologic Cycle*
  - *Make the Water Cycle*

Procedure

1. Hand out *Make the Water Cycle* worksheet. Write the vocabulary words on the board. The correct definitions are in the *Glossary*. Use your own methods to explain the words to the students and drill them on pronunciation.

2. Hand out the *Hydrologic Cycle* worksheet, and explain the four steps of the cycle. Hand out the *Make the Water Cycle* worksheet and review the instructions and safety procedures regarding the safe use of the electric burners.

3. Have your students follow the instructions on the worksheet. Supervise the students to prevent problems and maintain order.

4. Within ten minutes, all students should have achieved the complete water cycle, in which the evaporating water forms steam which condenses against the cold aluminum pie plate, resulting in precipitation.

5. Have the students complete their worksheets. Ask them what they observed. Ask them to discover how the cycle relates to their everyday lives.

Extensions/Modifications

- This activity can be done as a demonstration if your students shouldn't use burners or if you don't have enough burners for the entire class.
- Another version of this lesson can be done without burners. Use clear glass or plastic cups. Pour water into the cups or cover with clear plastic wrap secured with a rubber band. Set the cups in the sun. After about 15 minutes, students will observe condensation on the sides of the cup and on the plastic wrap. Precipitation may also be observed, depending on the heat of the day. Placing ice on the plastic wrap will increase the likelihood of precipitation.

Although students will probably not observe evaporation, explain to them that it must happen for the water to condense along the sides of the cup.

- For ESL students, translate the vocabulary words into their language and have all the students learn both sets of words.

Answers to the fill-in questions on the *Make the Water Cycle* worksheet:

1. Water in its solid state is called <u>ice.</u>

2. Water <u>evaporates</u> when it is heated.

3. Rain is another word for <u>precipitation.</u>

4. Clouds are formed by <u>condensation.</u>

5. Water <u>accumulates</u> in oceans, lakes and rivers.

Make the Water Cycle

Name: _____

Materials

❏ Portable electric burner

❏ Pot of water

❏ Aluminum pie plate

❏ Ice

❏ Pot holders or mittens

Instructions

Be very careful when handling the electric burner. It will get very hot, and can cause burns.

1. Plug in the electric burner, or have your teacher do it. Set the heat to medium-high.

2. Place a pot half full of water on the burner.

3. Place ice in your pie plate.

4. When the water begins to heat and you can see steam starting to rise from it, place your pie plate with ice about 12" (1/3 meter) above the pot. You will have to hold it there for a few minutes.

5. After a few minutes, you will see the hydrologic cycle at work! Water evaporates as steam from the pot. When it reaches the cold pie plate, it condenses on the bottom of the plate. You may even see a cloud of steam forming under the pie plate.

6. After a few minutes more, you will see that the water condensing on the pie plate forms large water drops. These drops are so heavy that they fall. You now have precipitation. See if you can direct the drips of water back into the pot of water where they accumulate, or gather. You have now completed the water cycle.

Fill in the correct words in the sentences:

1. Water in its solid state is called _____

2. Water _____ when it is heated.

3. Rain is another word for _____

4. Clouds are formed by _____

5. Water _____ in oceans, lakes and rivers.

The Hydrologic Cycle

*Name:*_____

Water is recycled again and again in the hydrologic cycle. Water accumulates, or gathers, in lakes and oceans. On a hot day, the water reaches its vapor point and evaporates into the air. This gas travels upward until it reaches a cold thermal layer above the earth. The coldness of the ice causes the warm gaseous water to cool and become liquid. This process is called condensation. Clouds are the result of condensation. As more water vapor condenses at the cold thermal layer, the water particles become large and heavy. These water molecules eventually fall out of the sky as rain. This is called precipitation.

Fill in the blanks to complete all four stages of the hydrologic cycle.
One of the stages is filled in for you.

2. It's Only A Leaky Faucet!

Subjects:
Science, Math, Social Studies

Process Skills:
Estimation, testing a hypothesis, conducting an experiment, recording data, measuring, use of conversion table, multiplication

Grades:
4–6

Cognitive Task Level:
Average

Time for Activity:
15 to 20 minutes

Key Vocabulary:
Faucet, precision, waste

Intended Learning Outcomes:
Completing this activity will allow students to:
- Observe and record how much water can be wasted from a leaky faucet
- Use basic math skills in problem solving
- Realize the power of the individual in making a significant difference in water conservation.

Background

Water is precious, but we are often careless about conserving it. Leaky faucets are a major source of unnecessary water loss. By becoming aware of this problem, students may be able to identify leaky faucets at home and elsewhere, and alert an adult to repair the problem.

Materials

- ❏ 8 oz. or 9 oz clear plastic cups (two cups for each pair of students)
- ❏ Measuring cups and teaspoons
- ❏ Clock
- ❏ Sink with faucet
- ❏ Handout:
  - *How Much Water Is Wasted From a Leaky Faucet?*

Procedure

1. Hand out the worksheet. Ask students: "How much water is wasted from a dripping faucet in one hour?" Have them write their guesses on their worksheets.

2. Form groups of students. Station each group at a water faucet. If you only have one faucet in the classroom, assign two students from each group to go to the faucet at a time. One student is the timekeeper and must tell the other student when to start and when to stop. Set the faucet to a moderate drip.

3. Instruct students to place their cups under the faucet and collect the drips for two minutes. Have them measure the number of teaspoons of water they collected. They should record this on their data sheets.

4. Multiply the number of teaspoons by 30 to determine the number of teaspoons of water wasted per hour. Using the conversion table provided, convert teaspoons to cups or quarts of water. Have the students compare their answers with their guesses. Did they guess high or low?

5. The numbers for each group will be slightly different. Ask them why this might be. The faucet drips at a different speed for each group. Select one group to give you its number, or use an average for the whole class, and finish the math on the board.

6. Multiply the number of cups per hour by 24 hours. Convert the number to gallons using the conversion table. Multiply the number of gallons of water wasted in one day by 30 to get the amount wasted in a month, and by 365 to get the amount wasted in one year.

7. Ask the students if they are surprised how much water can be wasted by one leaky faucet. Then ask, "How much water would be wasted every hour if everyone in the class had a dripping faucet? How much water would be wasted if the water was dripping twice as fast?"

8. Help your students think of ways to let people know about the problem of leaky faucets. Take an active role in helping them write notes to neighbors, make signs, or start a water patrol.

Extensions/Modifications

- Have students collect drips for five minutes as well as two minutes. After multiplying each by the correct amount to get an hour's worth of drips, see if the numbers match. Which number would be more precise? The data collected over the longer period should be more precise.
- Have students measure their water in metric containers, and compare these figures to the U.S. standard measurements. If you have students from another country in your class, ask them what methods of measurement are used in their country.

How Much Water is Wasted From a Leaky Faucet

Name _____

Conversions:

     3 teaspoons (tsp) = 1 tablespoon
     5 tablespoons (Tbsp) = 1/4 cup
     20 Tbsp = 1 cup
     4 cups = 1 quart
     4 quarts = 1 gallon

How much water do you think will leak from the faucet in one hour?
Write your guess here. _____

Instructions

1.   Set the faucet at a moderate drip.

2.   Place your cup under the faucet and have someone carefully watch the time.

3.   After 2 minutes, remove your cup.

4.   Using a teaspoon, take the water from the cup and put it into an empty cup. Count how many teaspoons of water you have. Answer the following question.

    How many teaspoons dripped from your faucet in two minutes? _____

5.   Multiply the number of teaspoons of water you had by 30. This tells you how many teaspoons of water are wasted in one hour. Write your answer here. _____

6.   Using the conversion table above, convert teaspoons to cups. If necessary, convert cups to quarts.

    Was your guess greater or less than the actual amount of water wasted? _____

7.   How much water can be wasted at one dripping faucet in one day? _____

    _____

    In one year? _____

3. How Much Water Do You Use?

Background

The more humans there are, the more water we need. Unnecessary water waste can be reduced with simple steps. In this activity students carry a *Water Use Record* with them for at least one day. They make an entry every time they use water, and then calculate the average number of gallons of water used each day. The *Reduce Water Waste!* handout gives students the opportunity to make decisions about changes they plan to make in their water use habits.

Subjects:
Science, Mathematics, Social Studies, Health, Art

Process Skills:
Counting, recording, addition and multiplication, estimation

Grades:
3 and above

Cognitive Task Level:
Average

Time for Activity:
Two 15-minute class periods, and homework

Key Vocabulary:
Conservation, consumption, reduce, waste

Intended Learning Outcomes:
Completing this activity will allow students to:
- Keep a diary of their own water use, calculate daily totals and make choices about where they can reduce water usage in their own lives
- Learn how much water they actually use and how they can reduce consumption.

Materials
❑ Handouts:
- *Personal Water Use Diary*
- *Reduce Water Waste!*

Procedure

1. Discuss water conservation with your students. We can reduce water by taking shorter showers, flushing the toilet only when necessary or turning off the faucet when brushing our teeth.

2. Have students bring in pictures of how humans use water in homes, and in all ways water is used. Post these on a bulletin board to remind students of the amount of water we use.

3. Hand out the *Personal Water Use Diary* and letter for their parents. Consider wording it as follows: "In class, we are studying water use and water conservation. Your child has a homework assignment to record the amount of water used in your house. To help him/her complete this homework assignment on how much water we all use, please share any water use that affects the student, such as washing clothes or dishes, watering the lawn or washing sidewalks or the car. Thanks for your help with this unit on water conservation!" Tell your students to show their parents the letter, and ask that the entire family inform your student if they use water in any way that affects the student, such as to water plants or the lawn, do laundry or run the dishwasher.

4. Have students keep their water record for one day. Include water used during school hours.

5. When the students have finished recording water use for one day, have them complete the math as a homework assignment. Don't forget to complete one yourself! When they return to class, have the students post the *Total Water Use* numbers on the board. Discuss the areas where they used the most water, and help them come up with ideas on how they can reduce their use of water.

6. Hand out the *Reduce Water Waste* handout, and have them put an X next to five actions they are willing to take to reduce water waste. Have each student write down at least one water-saving idea at the bottom of the page. Ask them if they really will do what they say they will. Follow up a few days later by asking them what they have done to reduce water waste. Be sure to tell them something that you have done as well.

Extensions/Modifications

- Make a bar graph with the Total Water Use numbers from your students. Look for the average amount of water used. Compare the person who used the most water with the one who used the least. Discuss why answers vary. Some students may have been better at recording their water use than others. Using an average figure removes the variation in the answers.

- Have your students keep their water records for two or three days, or over the weekend. When they bring the diary back to school, have them determine the average water use per day and the greatest use of water in the family. Ask them to focus on ways to reduce that area of water waste.

Personal Water Use Diary

Name _____

Mark the proper space every time you use water. When you go home, ask your family members to tell you any time they use water in any way that affects you, such as to water plants or the lawn, do laundry or run the dishwasher.

The column labeled Average Amounts helps you to make your own estimate, using the average water flow. If you have a low-flow shower head, your average is two gallons per minute.

Activity	Average Amounts	Time (Minutes)	Number of Times Per Day	Total Water Use
Taking a bath	25 gallons/ bath or 5 gallons/ minute			
Taking a shower	50 gallons/ shower or 5 gallons/ minute			
Flushing a toilet	5 gallons			
Washing face or hands	2 gallons or 5 gallons/ minute			
Brushing teeth	1/4 gallon or 5 gallons/ minute			
Washing clothes	40 gallons/ load			
Using a dishwashing machine	10 gallons/ load			
Watering plants	5 gallons/ minute			
Using the sprinkler	10 gallons/ minute			
Other uses				

Reduce Water Waste

Name _____

Mark an X next to five things you think you can do to reduce the amount of water you waste.

_____ Shower for five minutes or less

_____ Place a bucket in the shower to collect water while it warms up. Use it to water plants.

_____ Seek out leaky faucets and get them repaired.

_____ Have your parents purchase low-flow shower heads for your showers and sinks.

_____ Only flush the toilet when you absolutely need to.

_____ Turn off the water when brushing your teeth or washing your face.

_____ When showering, turn off the water while you soap your body, turn it on to rinse off.

_____ Take a sponge bath in the bathtub with the least amount of water possible.

_____ Use water from boiling or steaming vegetables to water plants.

_____ When washing the car, use an automatic shut-off nozzle to reduce water loss.

_____ Water lawns in the morning or evening to reduce evaporation.

_____ Use a broom rather than a hose to clean off walkways and patios.

_____ Ask your family and friends to use less water.

What other ways can we reduce water waste? Write your answers here.

_____

_____

_____

_____

_____

_____

4. Water Words Puzzle

Subjects:
Science, Language Arts, Social Studies

Process Skills:
Writing, reading, deciphering clues, communicating

Grades:
4-6

Cognitive Task Level:
Average to difficult

Time for Activity:
20 minutes

Intended Learning Outcomes:
Completing this activity will allow students to:
- Practice using vocabulary words from this unit
- Test their understanding of water conservation words and concepts
- Practice deciphering clues and finding hidden words.

Materials
❑ Handouts:
- *Water Words Fill-In*
- *Water Words Scramble*

Procedure

1. After completing the other lessons in this unit, hand out this fun activity for your students to assess their understanding and knowledge of the words and concepts that were presented in the unit. The words are hidden in the puzzle. The students can approach the puzzle in one of two ways. They can first look for the words hidden in the puzzle, and then answer the questions, or they can answer the questions first, and then look for those words in the puzzle.

2. Reward the students who finish first, and check their words. Go over the puzzle together after everyone has finished.

Extensions/Modifications
- To make the puzzle easier, list the words on the board so that students know what words to look for.
- To expand on the lesson, make the puzzle a homework assignment and require your students to write sentences using the words in proper context.
- For ESL classes, have the students learn the words in both languages.

Resources for Water Conservation
Books for Adults
- *Biology Concepts and Applications*, by Cecie Starr. Wadsworth Publishing Company.
- *Earth in the Balance*, by Al Gore. Plume. This book provides information about the present environmental concerns we face. Well-written and concise.
- *Graywater Use in the Landscape*, by Edible Publications. This booklet provides a concise and comprehensive discussion of the value and practical applications of installing a graywater system.
- *Plumbing*. Time-Life Books.

Books for Students
- *The Magic School Bus at the WaterWorks*, by Joanna Cole. Scholastic Inc. This book explains how the water cycle works as well as how water is treated before it comes through the faucet.
- *The Science Book of Water*, by Neil Ardley. Harcourt Brace Jovanovich. This beautifully photographed book provides simple water experiments that can be done at home or in the classroom.
- *Sea Otters*, by Marianne Reidman. Monterey Bay Aquarium Foundation. Contains information about sea otters and river otters, and presents career opportunities in biology.
- *50 Simple Things You Can Do to Save the Earth*, by The Earthworks Group. Earthworks Press.

Water Words Fill-In

Name _____

Answer the questions by filling in the blank words.
Then find the words in the Water Words Scramble.

1. When your faucet is dripping water, it has a _____.

2 Most of our drinking water comes from _____.

3. When water is heated, it will _____.

4. If you don't take a bath, you probably take a _____.

5. This word means water. It is also a color. _____.

6. Rain is another word for _____.

7. Frozen water is called _____.

8. When there is not enough water, we are in a _____.

9. Clouds are formed by _____.

10. Water is stored in _____.

11. The North Pole has water stored as _____.

12. Salt water is found in the _____.

13. When there is too much water in the clouds, it falls to the ground as_____.

14. Using more water than you need to is _____.

15. We can learn to _____ the amount of water we use.

16. We need to _____ lots of fresh, clean water every day.

Name _____

```
P X W A S T E F U L A Z B Y
R E S E R V O I R S S C V D
E F U R G I M C P Q H D O O
C O N D E N S A T I O N C S
I E A R Q C X E R T W X E N
P V X O T L Y U I O E P A A
I A S U D E F G L D R I N K
T P K G L A C I E R S H R G
A O Z H X K C C V A N M E W
T R E T A S D E F I C X D Z
I A Q S X C D E R N V T U G
O T P A Q U A N I J B U C Y
N E X G R O U N D W A T E R
```

Answers to *Water Words Fill-In*

1. When your faucet is dripping water, it has a <u>leak.</u>

2. Most of our drinking water comes from <u>groundwater.</u>

3. When water is heated, it will <u>evaporate.</u>

4. If you don't take a bath, you probably take a <u>shower.</u>

5. This word means water. It is also a color. <u>Aqua</u>

6. Rain is another word for <u>precipitation.</u>

7. Frozen water is called <u>ice.</u>

8. When there is not enough water, we are in a <u>drought.</u>

9. Clouds are formed by <u>condensation.</u>

10. Water is stored in <u>reservoirs.</u>

11. The North Pole has water stored as <u>glaciers.</u>

12. Salt water is found in the <u>oceans.</u>

13. When there is too much water in the clouds, it falls to the ground as <u>rain.</u>

14. Using more water than you need to is <u>wasteful.</u>

15. We can learn to <u>reduce</u> the amount of water we use.

16. We need to <u>drink</u> lots of fresh, clean water every day.

Answers to *Water Words Scramble*

```
P X W A S T E F U L X X X X
R E S E R V O I R S S X X X
E X X X X X X X X H X O X
C O N D E N S A T I O N C X
I E X R X X X X X W X E X
P V X O X L X X X X E X A X
I A X U X E X X X D R I N K
T P X G L A C I E R S X R X
A O X H X K X C X A X X E X
T R X T X X X E X I X X D X
I A X X X X X X X N X X U X
O T X A Q U A X X X X X C X
N E X G R O U N D W A T E R
```

Water Quality

The Challenge

Clean water contains hydrogen and oxygen. It becomes polluted when toxins, or poisons, get into the water. Pollutants can be industrial chemicals, fertilizers, wastes, biological contaminants (like bacteria or viruses), gasoline or sediment. Poisons even stick to a speck of soil as it runs into the water. Pollutants get into the water directly, through pipes, or they seep in through the ground.

When water is polluted, it can make humans, animals and plants sick. We can't survive without fresh, clean water. Most of the time in this country, we don't think about pollution. We believe the water at the kitchen sink is clean. But sometimes, we may have to boil our water before we can drink it, just to keep from becoming sick from it.

We don't have to drink polluted water. We purify our water in treatment plants, and nature also recycles water through the natural cycle. That way, it's clean enough for us to use again. We can also try to keep pollutants from getting into the water in the first place.

The Water Quality chapter of the *Animal Tracks Activity Guide* corresponds to the Pelican chapter of the *Animal Tracks* children's book.

Did You Know?

- There are five to six million storage tanks buried underground in the United States. Many hold gasoline, and 10,000 are estimated to leak.
- Pollution in the ocean kills fish and wildlife. Sea turtles die eating plastic bags. Toxic chemicals flow into the ocean in rain and as runoff, or are dumped from ships. Sewage fertilizes algae, which grows fast, choking the water. Fish then smother without oxygen.
- Drinking water can be treated by adding air to it, running it through filters or by adding cleansing chemicals to it.
- Wetlands are natural treatment plants! These marshy places prevent soil erosion and can actually clean water.

1. Soil Permeability and Toxic Chemicals

Subjects:
Science, Social Studies, Soil Science, Health, Language Arts

Process Skills:
Reading and following instructions, team building, observing, testing, analyzing results, writing, discussion

Grades:
3–6

Cognitive Task Level:
Average

Time for Activity:
25 to 30 minutes

Key Vocabulary:
Contaminant, erosion, groundwater, permeability, run-off, toxic, chemical

Intended Learning Outcomes:
Completing this activity will allow students to:

- Understand that materials can be picked up by water and transported through soil
- Observe that different types of soil have different physical qualities
- Learn about soil composition, permeability and run-off, and how these factors contribute to pollution in our drinking water.

Background

When toxic chemicals contaminate our drinking water, the health of an entire community is endangered. Seemingly benign behavior — such as dumping used motor oil or paint thinner onto the ground — can have potentially serious consequences if the pollutant is carried into the drinking water supply. This non-point contamination occurs either by percolating into the soil or as run-off during a strong rain. This lesson illustrates two ways that toxic chemicals can enter lakes and aquifers. The first activity demonstrates the different permeability characteristics of soil, and the second shows how run-off occurs, and illustrates the damage caused by erosion. Placing a "toxin" (red food color) in the soil illustrates how toxics get into the groundwater and drinking water supplies.

Materials

For soil erosion activity (one for each set of students):

- ❑ Shoe box
- ❑ 3 small bags of soil collected from the school yard
- ❑ Large handful of fresh grass or other green waste
- ❑ Large watering can full of water
- ❑ Red food coloring
- ❑ Handout:
  - • *Soil Erosion Experiment* worksheet

For soil permeability activity (one for each set of students):

- ❑ 2 large pans to catch water
- ❑ 2 similar-sized coffee cans with 8 to 10 holes punched in the bottom
- ❑ 2 cups of water
- ❑ Watch to count minutes and seconds
- ❑ 2 types of soil, enough of each to half-fill the cans:
  - ❑ Sand or gravel
  - ❑ Potting soil
- ❑ Handout:
  - • *Soil Permeability Experiment* worksheet

Procedure

1. Divide the class into groups of six students. Each group will conduct both experiments. Three students will do the soil permeability experiment; the other three will do the soil run-off experiment. Be sure you have enough materials for all groups.

2. Distribute the worksheets for the two activities.

3. While the students are preparing for the soil permeability experiment, place several drops of red food coloring into one of the two containers of soil each group is using. Don't let the students know which container it's in. Place red dye into every box used by the group conducting the soil erosion experiment.

4. Have the students complete the experiments and answer the questions on the worksheets. When they have finished their experiments, have the students who conducted one experiment explain to the other students in their group what they learned.

5. Start a discussion about the results of the experiments. Were the students surprised by the results? How do they feel about dumping toxic materials in the soil now?

6. Have your students write a story about toxic chemicals and their effect on water and soil. Ask them to explain what might happen to plants and animals that live in the soil. Encourage them to be creative. Have them include an idea on how to prevent or solve this problem.

Extensions/Modifications

- • These two experiments can also be done as demonstrations for the class.
- • The soil permeability experiment can be done by using one type of soil. You can also conduct the experiment without the data sheets, and follow up the activity with a discussion of the observations the students made.
- • For a more complex version of the soil permeability activity, use four different types of soil: gravel, sand, potting soil and clay. Conduct the experiment for each, and compare the speed at which water travels through each.

Soil Permeability Experiment

Name _____

Materials Needed

❑ Large pans to catch water
❑ 2 similar-sized coffee cans with 8 to 10 holes punched in the bottom
❑ 2 cups of water
❑ Watch to count minutes and seconds
❑ 2 types of soil, enough of each to half-fill the cans:
   ❑ Sand or gravel
   ❑ Potting soil

Instructions

1. Fill each can half full with a different type of soil. Each type of soil allows water to move through it at a different speed. The speed that water passes through soil indicates its *permeability*.

2. Write the name of the soil you *think* is most permeable. The water will pass faster through the more permeable soil. My prediction is _____.

3. Place the can of soil over the pan, and pour the cup of water into the can. Have one person be the timer, and time how long it takes for the first drips of water to reach the pan. Time how long it takes for all the water to reach the pan. If the water has not stopped dripping after five minutes, stop timing.

Type of soil: _____

Time elapsed until first sign of water:_____

Time elapsed until all the water drips through: _____

Type of soil: _____

Time elapsed until first sign of water:_____

Time elapsed until all the water drips through: _____

Which soil was the most permeable? _____

Was your prediction correct?_____

Soil Erosion Experiment

Name _____

Materials Needed

❑   2 large pans to catch water
❑   Shoe box
❑   3 small bags of soil collected from the school yard
❑   Large handful of fresh grass or other green waste
❑   Large watering can full of water
❑   Red food coloring

Instructions

1.   This experiment will show how water travels over soil when grass is present and when it is absent. Place the dirt in the shoe box. Mound the dirt on one end so it's higher than the other, like a small hill. Place the shoe box over a large pan. Pour water over the higher end fairly fast and let it drain into the pan.

2.   Place the shoe box over the second pan. Place the green grasses on top of the soil. Pour water over the higher end and let the water collect in the pan.

3.   Answer the following questions:
Which pan is muddier, which means it has the most soil in it? _____
_____

Which one had the least? _____
_____

When soil washes away with water in a storm, it may result in *erosion*. From what you observed, how can you prevent erosion? _____
_____

What happened to the red dye your teacher placed in the soil? _____
_____

What might have happened if this dye had been toxic? _____
_____

2. Be a Water Treatment Officer

Subjects:
Science, Social Studies, Geography, Health

Process Skills:
Reading and following directions, observing results, hands-on manipulation, problem solving, developing vocabulary

Grades:
4–6

Cognitive Task Level:
Average

Time for Activity:
30 to 40 minutes

Key Vocabulary:
Aerate, aquifer, bacteria, coagulation, chlorinate, filtration, microorganisms, reservoir, sedimentation

Intended Learning Outcomes:
Completing this activity will allow students to:

- Explain the steps and processes involved in purifying water at a water treatment plant
- Understand why water must be cleansed and purified before it is safe for human consumption
- Discover where the sources of drinking water occur in the area
- Recognize a career option that connects environmental and health issues in a way that directly benefits society.

Background

When water falls to earth and flows into reservoirs, aquifers and lakes, it collects dirt particles, bacteria or pollutants. These contaminants must be removed before our water is safe to drink. This activity simulates the treatment process water goes through before it flows from our tap.

The United States has one of the best and cleanest drinking water systems in the world. Water is first aerated, by spraying it into the air to release trapped gasses and to absorb oxygen. Next, powdered alum is added to the water. This binds to dirt particles suspended in the water (coagulation). The particles, now called "floc," become heavy and sink to the bottom (sedimentation). The water is then filtered through layers of sand, gravel and charcoal to remove the small particles. Finally, a small amount of chlorine is added to kill bacteria and microorganisms.

Materials
- ❑ 1-pound bag of clean aquarium gravel
- ❑ 1-pound bag of clean sand
- ❑ 1 container of powdered alum (found in the spice section of a grocery store)
- ❑ 2 clear plastic cups per team
- ❑ 1 polystyrene (Styrofoam) cup per team of students
- ❑ Paper towel cut in quarters
- ❑ Eyedropper filled with non-chlorine bleach mixed with water (to simulate chlorine)
- ❑ Large bucket of water with 1 cup of dirt mixed into it
- ❑ Large soup ladle (optional)
- ❑ Handouts
  - *The Water Treatment Plant*

Procedure

1. This activity works well with a discussion about aquifers and reservoirs. Ask students if they know the source of their local drinking water. Learn the name of the local reservoir or aquifer, and identify it on a local map. Some students may be revolted at the thought that their drinking water comes from a reservoir where boating and fishing activities also occur. Explain that water is treated before it reaches our faucets. Explain that during this activity they will become "water treatment officers" for a day, and learn how to properly treat water before it is released for consumption. Briefly explain how water is treated before starting the activity.

2. Break the class into groups of two to three students. Distribute *The Water Treatment Plant* handout, and ask students to consider the bucket of dirty water to be the reservoir. Instruct one student from each group to stir the water well with the soup ladle and use it to fill one clear plastic cup three-quarters full. Have the other students in the group collect the materials they need and set up the simulation activity.

3. Have the students follow the instructions on their *Water Treatment Plant* handout. Offer assistance if needed and keep order in the room. Supervise the activity as the students carry out their simulation.

Extensions/Modifications

- A simpler version of this activity is to use a coffee filter and a funnel. This illustrates how water is filtered without following the more complex instruction in this activity.

- Use the words in this lesson for vocabulary words of the week.

- Read *The Magic School Bus At The Waterworks* By Joanna Cole, or assign the book as homework reading. It reinforces the concepts presented here.

- Take your students on a field trip to see how a real water treatment plant functions. Or take them to the wastewater treatment plant, which handles water from homes, drains and restrooms. Have a representative from your local water treatment facility speak to your class about water treatment.

The Water Treatment Plant

Name _____

Instructions

1. Take one clear plastic cup to the "reservoir" and fill it three-quarters full of water.

2. Using a pencil, punch eight to ten holes in the bottom of the white foam cup. Place a piece of paper towel or filter paper on the bottom of the cup. Put one inch of gravel in the cup. Cover the gravel with one inch of sand. Set this filter cup aside.

3. Pour the dirty water in the clear cup into the other clear cup. Repeat two more times. This step is called *aeration*.

4. Take 1/2 tsp. alum and put it into the cup with water. The alum will bind to the dirt. This is called *coagulation*. The alum and dirt are heavy and will form a layer on the bottom of the cup. This is called *sedimentation*.

5. Place an empty cup underneath the white foam cup with the sand and gravel filter. After the particles in the clear cup have fallen to the bottom, pour the water into the white foam cup. This step is called *filtration*. The water coming through the filter is free of dirt.

6. Place two drops of non-chlorine bleach into the clean water. If this were really chlorine, it would kill bacteria and micro-organisms in the water. If this were a real water treatment plant, you would now have water clean enough to drink.

7. When cleaning up, save the water to water plants. Wash the clear plastic cups so they can be used again.

3. Adopt A Water Friend

Subjects:
Science, Social Studies, Language Arts, Health

Process Skills:
Identifying plants and animals, classifying, collecting and analyzing data, recording observations, taking temperature, measuring pH, writing reports, problem-solving

Grades:
4-8

Cognitive Task Level:
Difficult

Time for Activity:
Three 15-minute periods prior to the field trip; at least two hours for the field trip itself and one 30-minute period after the field trip

Key Vocabulary:
Aquatic life, pollution, wildlife, waterway, biotic assessment, pH, conservation

Intended Learning Outcomes:
Completing this activity will allow students to:
- Learn science and observation skills
- Recognize the value of conservation and habitat improvement
- Develop a sense of ownership for a natural area
- Demonstrate personal responsibility for improving water quality and reducing pollution
- Improve communication skills.

Background

Just as many cities have "adopt-a-highway" programs, students can adopt a water friend. By conducting a series of observations and recording their data, students can complete a modified version of a biotic assessment. Biotic assessments are studies conducted by biologists to determine the relative ecological health of an area by observing the number and diversity of plants and animals, checking the pH of water and soil and looking for the effect of human disturbance on an area. When completed, your class will have made a "biotic assessment" of their water friend and its immediate surroundings. The diversity and number of plants and animals and the amount of human impact serve as indicators of the biotic "health" of an area.

Your class can develop an action plan to conserve the area and, if necessary, help it recover from pollution or disturbance. Send a copy of the biotic assessment and action plan to a local environmental organization and the newspaper to help bring public attention to the area.

Materials
- ☐ Map of local area
- ☐ Thermometer
- ☐ Tape measure (10 feet)
- ☐ pH testing paper
- ☐ Field guides for plants and animals
- ☐ Large plastic bags for collecting litter
- ☐ Camera
- ☐ Handouts
  - *Adopt A Water Friend* data sheets

Procedure

1. A week or two before selecting your water friend, ask your students to find nearby areas where water occurs. Do they know of a creek, lake, park pond, stream or inlet to adopt? Have a map of your local area ready so that you can find the places your students suggest. Keep track of their suggestions. At the end of the week, list the places. Select a good site to adopt. A site within walking distance of the school is best; students can easily return to it later in the year.

Purchase pH paper from a swimming pool supply store, science supply catalog or hardware store. Be sure to buy pH paper that ranges from 1 to 15. Follow the directions for use on the container.

2. The day before your field trip, divide your students into their groups and tell them what their jobs will be at the site. Go over proper field trip etiquette and rules. Be sure they know what is expected of them. Remind them to wear sturdy shoes and bring jackets, if necessary. If you plan to stay for lunch, remind them to bring their lunches.

3. On the day of the field trip, give your students their data sheets and assignments. Have each group fill out their data sheets. Then, as a whole class, clean up the litter or remove other evidence of human use that you can.

4. When you return to the classroom, each group must complete a summary of what they found. Have your students work in their teams and write up a summary of what they discovered about the area (See example). One student may be selected to write the summary, or you may have each student write up their own summary. Take photographs of each team's area.

5. Place the students in groups so that each person in the group worked on a different part of the biotic assessment. Have the students read their summaries aloud to each other so that everyone learns about every activity. The combined information from all the summaries is similar to a completed biotic assessment of the area. As a class, decide whether the area you selected is a healthy one or not.

6. Develop an "action plan" which includes ideas for cleaning up and preserving your water friend. Some suggestions are as follows:

- Clean up the shoreline and help keep it clean on a regular basis.
- Find out what native plants would grow along your water friend and plant them in areas that suffer from erosion.
- Find out what kind of fish should be living in your stream, river, lake or ocean.
- Set up a pollution patrol to guard your water friend.

7. Send a copy of the biotic assessment and action plan to a local environmental organization and the newspaper to help bring public attention to the area.

8. Return to your water friend at the end of the school year. Take notes and photographs of any changes made to the area, or repeat the biotic assessment to determine what changes have occurred since the last visit.

Extensions/Modifications

- Invite a member of a local environmental organization to speak to the students about this body of water.
- Simplify the lesson by just asking students to observe their natural area and describe it.
- For more ideas on ways to expand on this lesson contact the following organizations:
  - For a stream, river or lake, you can write to The Izaak Walton League of America, 707 Conservation Lane, Gaithersburg, MD 20878. Ask for the kit to keep track of your stream's water quality.
  - For ocean conservation, contact The Center for Marine Conservation, 1725 De Sales St. NW, Washington DC 20036; 202-429-5609.
- Encourage your school or organization to adopt your water friend for at least five years. Keep a diary to evaluate the progress you make on a yearly basis. Try to keep the same students involved as well as bringing on new students to help.

Resources for Water Quality

Field Guides

- *Pond Life, A Golden Guide.* Golden Press. The Golden Guides are excellent for identifying the most commonly seen animals. Other good guides are *Insect, Reptiles and Amphibians, Mammals, Mushrooms, Flowers* and *Birds*.
- *A Field Guide to Animal Tracks,* by Olaus J. Murie. Houghton Mifflin Company. This excellent book, part of the Peterson Field Guide series, will tell you all you need to know to identify animal tracks.

Books for Students

- *Brown Pelican at the Pond,* by E. O'Reilly. Manzanita Press
- *Oil Spills: Danger in the Sea,* by Joseph E. Brown. Dodd, Mean and Co.

Books for Adults

- *Silent Spring,* by Rachel Carson. Houghton Mifflin Company. This was one of the first popular books to describe the problems associated with pollution and pesticides.
- *Plastics in the Ocean: More than a Litter Problem.* Center for Marine Conservation.
- *The Return of the Brown Pelican,* by J. Brown. Louisiana State University.

Adopt A Water Friend: Group 1 — Temperature

Using a thermometer, measure temperature in the following places:

IN THE WATER

Place the thermometer in water in a sunny spot and in a shady spot.

In the Sun _____

In the Shade_____

IN THE AIR

Hold the thermometer at chest height, away from your body. If it is windy, shield the thermometer from the wind.

In the Sun _____

In the Shade_____

IN THE SOIL

Place the thermometer base gently into the surface of the soil.

In the Sun _____

In the Shade_____

Adopt A Water Friend: Group 2 — Soil Moisture and pH

Collect soil samples in the following places.

Write a description of the soil. Is it like sand, or does it stick together like clay? Is it light brown, reddish or dark brown? Does it have a smell? Use other words to describe the soil.

At the water's edge: _____

_____

_____

5 feet away from the water in the sun: _____

_____

_____

5 feet away from the water in the shade: _____

_____

_____

Use pH paper to determine the pH of the water and of the soil:

pH of water: _____

pH of damp soil: _____

Adopt A Water Friend: Group 3 — Plants

Describe the plants at water's edge. Are there plants in the water? What do they look like? Are they mostly flowering plants, grasses, trees or shrubs? If you know what types of plants they are, write down their names. Use a field guide to identify as many plants as you can.

_____   _____

_____   _____

_____   _____

Describe the plants that are closest to the water but not in the water. Are they trees, grasses, shrubs or small flowers? How tall are they? Use the tape measure to measure their height, or estimate their height by comparing the height of the plants to a person. Describe one here or draw a picture of it. _____

_____

_____

Use the tape measure to get 10 feet away from the water. Describe the plants here. Are they the same as the ones at the water's edge? Describe them or draw a picture of them. _____

_____

_____

Adopt A Water Friend: Group 4 — Animals

Are there animals in the water? What are they? Fish, insects, frogs or toads are common water animals. Describe a water animal here. Draw a picture of it below. _____

_____

Keep a list of all the animals that your class sees on the field trip. You should be able to find at least five animals, and probably more. Look for birds, insects, squirrels, frogs, lizards, turtles or other animals. If you have a field guide, try to identify the animals. Write down animal tracks, too.

_____   _____

_____   _____

_____   _____

_____   _____

Adopt A Water Friend: Group 5 — Human Impact

Take "before" photographs of the site.

Write down your group's first impression of the area. Is it dirty? Is there a lot of litter and garbage around? Or is the site clean? _____

_____

_____

_____

_____

Record all evidence of humans here. Include graffiti, tire tracks and all pieces of litter that you find.

After your class has cleaned up the area, take an "after" photograph of the site. Write your impressions in a log that the teacher can keep from year to year. _____

_____

_____

_____

_____

_____

Air Quality

The Challenge

All of us — humans, plants and animals — need air to live. Clean air is a mix of gases that we can't see. Air is mostly nitrogen and oxygen.

For millions of years, the earth has had a good system to keep its air clean. Green plants are natural air filters. They use sunlight to convert water and carbon dioxide (CO_2) into the oxygen we breathe. The system worked well until we put so many pollutants into the air that the natural system couldn't handle them all.

We ruin those natural air filters when we cut and burn trees in the tropical rain forests. The burning of those trees releases carbon dioxide into our air instead of converting it. Too much carbon dioxide in our air can be harmful.

We also pollute our air with the exhaust from our vehicles, the smoke from burning coal and oil to make energy and the fumes from manufacturing and industry processes. We pollute with man-made products we use in our houses. Pollutants in the air can even cause water pollution, such as when acid rain falls from the sky into rivers and lakes.

The Air Quality chapter of the *Animal Tracks Activity Guide* corresponds to the Eagle chapter of the *Animal Tracks* children's book.

Did You Know?

- "Good ozone" in the upper atmosphere, 10 to 25 miles above earth, shields us from the sun's harmful ultraviolet rays.

- "Harmful ozone," which creates smog, occurs close to earth and is a mix of nitrogen oxide and hydrocarbons, primarily from car exhaust. It damages the leaves on plants and can cause breathing problems for humans.

- The average American car produces 7.5 tons of carbon dioxide every year. That's about one pound per mile.

- The average number of bicycle-riders who pass through a major intersection in New York City in one hour is 173. In Tianjin, China, it is 50,000. China suffers from pollution, but using bicycles instead of cars sure cuts down on pollution from vehicles!

- Indoor air pollution comes from tobacco smoke, cleaning compounds, heaters and even the walls. Plants like English ivy, pothos, schefflera and philodendron have proved to naturally help clean such pollution.

1. Pollution Collectors

Subjects:
Science, Environmental Science, Health

Process Skills:
Designing experiments, observing and recording results, analyzing results

Grades:
2–6

Cognitive Task Level:
Average

Time for Activity:
15 minutes to make collectors, 2 to 3 days to complete activity

Key Vocabulary:
Pollution, particles, pollutants

Intended Learning Outcomes:
Completing this activity will allow students to:
- Design a solid particle collector
- Collect and observe particles that occur in air
- Determine where air pollution occurs in greatest concentrations both indoors and outdoors.

Background

There are two kinds of air pollution: solid particles and gases. Solid particles may come from nature, such as pollen from flowers and trees, or dust from soil. Other particles are by-products of human activities, like burning trash, fuel combustion in automobiles and factories and even the rubber particles that erode from tires on a moving automobile. Although solid particles occur in all the air we breathe, we often are not aware of them until they can be observed in high concentration, like the dust that can be shaken from a dust mop, or the smoke that emerges from a chimney or smoke stack.

Our bodies are well adapted to deal with solid particles in air. We have hair in our noses and cilia lining our lungs. These are covered with a moist mucus, which collects particles and draws them out of the air. These natural air filters protect our delicate tissues from possibly hazardous pollutants.

This activity involves collecting and observing solid particles found in air. Be sure to have your students place their pollution collectors in a variety of places for this activity.

Materials

- ❑ Clear contact paper with a sticky side, or white paper cards and petroleum jelly
- ❑ Pieces of cardboard or chipboard (the composition of a cereal box)
- ❑ Thumbtacks or glue
- ❑ Magnifying glass or microscope
- ❑ Handout:
  - *Pollution Collectors*

Procedure

1. To make a pollution collector, cut the contact paper or white paper into two-inch by two-inch squares. Cut the cardboard into four-inch by four-inch squares. Mount the paper to the cardboard or chipboard base with glue. If using the contact paper, mount the contact paper sticky side out. If using the plain paper, smear a thin coating of petroleum jelly onto the surface of the paper. Have each student or team make three pollution collectors.

2. Decide where each collector will be placed. Discuss areas that your students think would have high quantities of particles, such as near a road, in a parking lot or near trees. Select other areas that would seem to have low concentrations of particles, such as in the house or bathroom or behind a wind break. Select at least one indoor site and one outdoor site. Label each collector, and include information about where it is placed. For example, label the card "school parking lot" or "Lisa's backyard."

3. Leave the particle collectors out for two or three days. Then, collect them. Be sure not to let them touch anything! Carefully place them in resealable plastic bags for transporting, if necessary.

4. Back in the classroom, have your students look at the collectors and place them in order from the dirtiest to the cleanest. Ask them to discern any patterns. Are the cards placed closer to streets dirtier than those in backyards? Have them describe the results on their *Pollution Collector* data sheets.

5. Use the magnifying lenses and microscopes to closely observe the dirt particles. Have them describe what they see.

6. Finish with a discussion about dirt particles in air and how they can become a problem when inhaled. The Teacher's Information Sheet on Air Pollution will provide you with more details about different types of pollutants. Ask your students if they knew that they inhaled these types of particles. Be sure to follow up the discussion with a talk about the natural protection mechanisms in our bodies. Nose hair and cilia on our lungs help filter particles, and sneezing is the body's way of expelling unwanted matter from the body. Ask your students what other types of body mechanisms help keep our bodies free from pollutants.

Extensions/Modifications

- This activity can be expanded by setting three collectors at each site. Leave one for one day, one for two days, and leave the last for three days. Compare the amount of particles on each collector.

- This activity can be expanded by taking some of the particles and placing them on agar solution, which can be purchased from science suppliers. Agar gel provides a proper environment for the growth of bacteria and fungi. Take the dirtiest particle collectors and stick them face down on the agar gel. Cover the gel and place in a warm area. If some of the particulate matter collected on the particle collectors are bacteria or fungi, these will grow and become visible in about a week. This can be used as a part of a discussion on the difference between natural solid particles, like molds, fungi or pollen, and man-made particles derived from burning coal. The latter particles will not grow fungi or bacteria.

Pollution Collectors

Name _____

Place your pollution collectors in three different locations. Write the locations below. After the experiment, rate what you found. Which site was dirtiest and which was cleanest?

Location	Level of Pollution (1 for the dirtiest; 3 for the cleanest)

Explain why the dirtiest location is so dirty, and why the cleanest location is cleanest. Write down an idea on how to make the dirtier location cleaner. _____

_____

_____

Pollution Collectors

Name _____

Place your pollution collectors in three different locations. Write the locations below. After the experiment, rate what you found. Which site was dirtiest and which was cleanest?

Location	Level of Pollution (1 for the dirtiest; 3 for the cleanest)

Explain why the dirtiest location is so dirty, and why the cleanest location is cleanest. Write down an idea on how to make the dirtier location cleaner. _____

_____

_____

Teacher's Information Sheet: Air Pollution

Use this information about air pollution to launch a discussion about solutions. Your students may come up with more ideas than are listed here. Encourage them to find solutions to those problems.

INDOORS:

1. Air conditioner: Contains chlorofluorocarbons in the refrigerant. Also mold and bacteria can grow in the moist spaces.
Solution: Use as little as possible. Have it checked regularly for leaks, clean the unit well with antibacterial cleaner.

2. Cigarette: Cigarettes contain 43 chemical compounds, many of which are toxic both to the smoker and anyone in the room.
Solution: Don't smoke.

3. Air deodorizer: Contributes chemicals that can irritate lungs and delicate nasal tissues.
Solution: Clean more often, open windows to clear a room.

4. Carpet and furniture: May contain formaldehyde and other poisonous chemicals.
Solution: Before buying new furnishings, ask if formaldehyde or other toxic chemicals have been used in its manufacture. If the answer is yes, keep the furniture outdoors or in a well-ventilated place for several days before using it. This will allow the chemicals to dissipate from the furniture.

5. Fireplace: Burning wood produces smoke, carbon dioxide and other chemicals that may be embedded in the wood.
Solution: Avoid lighting fires as much as possible. Avoid burning wood treated with chemicals, and keep your chimney clean and functioning properly.

6. Oven cleaner or other cleaning supplies: Contribute toxic chemicals.
Solution: Use non-toxic alternatives whenever possible. Open windows and doors when using the products. Wear gloves to prevent skin from absorbing chemicals.

7. Flea Bomb: Contains poisonous chemicals to kill fleas.
Solution: If possible, flea bomb no more than twice a year. Keep pets flea-free with frequent bathing and flea combing. Always air house well after bombing.

OUTDOORS:

1. Barbecue: Wood creates smoke; lighter fluid contributes dangerous chemicals.
Solution: Use lighter fluids as little as possible, barbecue less often, and cover after use.

2. Power Lawnmower: Gasoline-fueled lawnmowers contribute carbon dioxide and carbon monoxide into the air.
Solution: Use a hand mower. You reduce pollution and get exercise, too!

3. Airplanes: By burning fuel, jets and airplanes contribute carbon dioxide.
Solution: Travel less, encourage stricter standards on air emissions.

4. Factory smoke: Contributes many varieties of gases, depending on the factory.
Solution: As part of community effort, impose greater air controls, require better fuel efficiency to accomplish more work for less fuel use.

5. Automobiles: Contribute carbon monoxide and carbon dioxide. Cars are the single greatest contributors of carbon dioxide in the United States.
Solution: Drive less. Carpool whenever possible. Use public transportation, walk or ride a bicycle. The fewer vehicles on the road, the less pollution is created.

6. Buses: Most buses still burn gasoline or diesel, which contribute carbon dioxide and carbon monoxide.
Solution: Encourage the transit authority to convert buses to clean-burning natural gas.

7. Landfill: Contributes methane, a greenhouse gas.
Solution: Produce less garbage, collect methane and burn for fuel.

8. Airplane spraying insecticide on field: Both the nitrogen fertilizer on the field and the airborne pesticide are air pollutants.
Solution: Use less fertilizer and pesticide, or buy organically grown foods that do not use chemical fertilizers or pesticides.

2. World Air Currents: How They Get Around

Subjects:
Environmental Science, Language Arts, Health

Process Skills:
Identifying sources, grouping, identifying solutions

Grades:
2–6

Cognitive Task Level:
Average

Time for Activity:
30 minutes

Key Vocabulary:
Indoor air pollution, particles, pollutants, gases

Intended Learning Outcomes:
Completing this activity will allow students to:
* Identify sources of pollution both indoors and outdoors
* Learn about different types of pollutants
* Identify solutions to common pollution problems.

Background

One of the reasons that air pollution is a global concern is that air travels throughout the world. Pollution that occurs in one country can travel on air currents and create problems for other countries.

Differences in the earth's temperature cause pressure gradients. As air moves from areas of high pressure to areas of low pressure, winds are created. Prevailing winds are winds that always blow in the same direction. The trade winds and westerly winds are prevailing winds. In the northern hemisphere, the westerly winds blow from the east to the west, from Eurasia across the Pacific Ocean to North America, and across North America and the Atlantic to Europe. The trade winds blow in a westerly direction, from northern Africa to Central America and from Central America across the Pacific to Asia and Indonesia. The overall pattern resembles a clockwise, circular flow of air over each of the two oceans, and a strong flow from west to east over the United States. These winds are so strong and constant that they drive the water currents as well. It was Christopher Columbus' understanding of wind and water currents that led him to believe that he could travel from Spain to the Orient. And he would have, except that America got in the way!

By using an overhead master of world air currents and a world map, teachers can stimulate discussion about world air pollution.

Materials
❑   Handout
   • *World Air Currents*

Procedure

1. Make an overhead master of the diagrammed world air currents. Display the diagram and use it as a source for discussion of air pollution. Explain how the combined effect of the prevailing westerly winds and the trade winds creates a circular pattern in the oceans between the continents. Winds from Russia blow over Alaska and across North America. Water currents are also sent from Russia to North America and then travel south along the coast to Baja California. The trade winds move air from Central America to Japan and Asia. The clockwise flow in the northern hemisphere and the counterclockwise flow in the southern hemisphere is due to a natural phenomenon called the Coriolis effect.

2. Test your students' understanding by quizzing them with the questions on air currents found on page 11. Use the world map to locate the places in the questions, then trace the currents on the overhead transparency with a marker.

Extensions/Modifications
* Expand this lesson to include discussion of water currents and their role in ocean pollution. A book on oceanography will provide a list of water currents.

World Air Currents

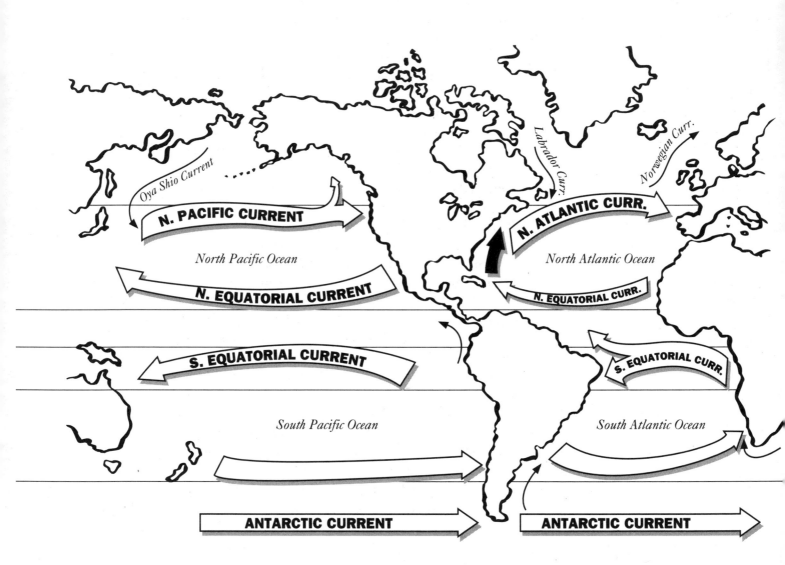

Air Currents Questions

Question: A bald eagle born in Alaska leaves its nest and is caught in a large storm. Where might that eagle end up?

Answer: The eagle would follow prevailing winds and could end up in British Columbia, Washington, Oregon, Idaho, Montana or California. In fact, this is part of the bald eagle's natural range. Further eastern movement may be blocked by the Rocky Mountains. By understanding the prevailing wind currents, your class should be able to accurately predict the correct range for the national bird.

Q: If a tropical storm began in the Gulf of Mexico, where would it go?

A: The trade winds move from the Equator north along the coast of North America. You can expect that storm to hit the southern United States in places such as Louisiana, Florida or South Carolina.

Q: High levels of carbon dioxide are produced by factories in Chicago, Illinois. This carbon dioxide causes acid rain to fall where?

A: Following the direction of the prevailing westerly winds, your students should predict that the acid rain would fall on the Great Lakes area, the northeastern most states and Canada.

Q: A nuclear power plant in Chernobyl, a town in eastern Russia exploded in April, 1986. Even after the reactor was shut down, trace amounts of atomic particles were caught in the winds and carried hundreds of miles away. Although the majority of the radioactive gases remained right around Chernobyl and eastern Europe, one cloud was caught in the prevailing westerly winds. Where would you expect to find some radioactive particles?

A: Caught in the prevailing westerly winds, trace amounts of radioactive particles traveled all the way across Russia and were detected in the state of Washington a month later.

Q: True or False: "We all live downwind."
A: True!

3. About The Atmosphere

Subjects:
Environmental Science, Math, Meteorology

Process Skills:
Linking concepts, designing models, using proportions

Grades:
3–6

Cognitive Task Level:
Average

Time for Activity:
30 minutes

Key Vocabulary:
Atmosphere, ozone, troposphere, mesosphere, stratosphere, thermosphere

Intended Learning Outcomes:
Completing this activity will allow students to:
- Learn about the composition of the atmosphere
- Develop an understanding of proportions
- Complete a scale drawing of the different levels of the atmosphere.

Background
When trying to understand air quality, it is necessary to learn how our atmosphere works. Each atmospheric layer has unique qualities. This activity requires students to draw a model of the earth's atmospheric layers in their correct proportions. Then they show where good ozone and bad ozone are found, where carbon dioxide molecules accumulate, where airplanes fly and where meteors are observed. They also learn about the roots of words used in the study of meteorology. They can be used by the teacher for developing vocabulary.

Materials
- ❑ Handouts
  - *The Earth's Atmosphere Instructions*
  - *The Earth's Atmosphere Map*
- ❑ Crayons or colored pencils
- ❑ Ruler
- ❑ Drawing compasses (optional)

Procedure
1. Describe the general idea of the atmosphere to your students. Use the teacher's version of the worksheet to explain the different levels of the atmosphere. This can be made into an overhead master to use as a teaching guide.

2. Hand out the Earth's Atmosphere worksheets and explain the proportional relationships. Explain that one inch represents ten miles of air. To make a correct model, students must understand the proportional relationship described in the worksheet.

3. Instruct your students to use the instruction sheet to draw the earth's atmosphere layers on the map. Be sure they identify where weather occurs, where planes usually fly and where meteors occur.

4. Encourage your students to color their completed pictures of the earth's atmosphere.

Extensions/Modifications
- To simplify this activity, make the first layer (troposphere) 10 miles thick. The actual troposphere varies in thickness.
- For younger students, draw the lines for the layers of the earth's atmosphere and have students label atmospheres and activities only.

Resources for Air Quality
- *Air*, by Robyn Freedman Spizman and Marianne Daniels Garber. Good Apple.
- *Pollution: Problems and Solutions*, by Ranger Rick's NatureScopes. National Wildlife Federation.
- *Fight Global Warming: 29 Things You Can Do*, by Sarah Clark. Environmental Defense Fund.
- *The Audubon Society Field Guide to the Bald Eagle*, by David Gordon. Sasquatch Books.
- *Kidsnet*, a computerized acid rain information exchange program. National Geographic Society.
- *Citizens Acid Rain Monitoring Group*. National Audubon Society.

The Earth's Atmosphere Instructions

1. Can you map this?

Draw the four layers of the earth's atmosphere in their correct proportions. Use the key below to guide you.

One inch equals ten miles

First Layer: Troposphere — Closest to the earth, it's between 6 and 12 miles thick. (Average = 10 miles)

Second Layer: Stratosphere — 20 miles thick.

Third Layer: Mesosphere — 20 miles thick.

Fourth Layer: Thermosphere — Starts 50 miles above the earth and fades into space.

2. What belongs there?

Place these in the correct atmospheric layer.

Weather: Most storms and clouds occur in the troposphere.

Jets: Jet airplanes fly in the troposphere above the clouds and storms.

Meteors: Most meteor trails, like that left by Halley's Comet, occur in the mesosphere.

Ozone: "Good" ozone occurs in the stratosphere. It protects the earth from ultraviolet rays. "Harmful" ozone occurs in the troposphere. It is a pollutant and occurs in smog. Draw "good" ozone into the stratosphere and "harmful" ozone in the troposphere.

Carbon Dioxide: This is found in high concentrations in the troposphere. Carbon dioxide absorbs heat from the sun, keeping our planet warm. Excessive build-up of carbon dioxide and carbon monoxide lead to global warming.

3. What do those words mean?

Many of the English words we use today come from ancient Greek and Latin languages. Find out about the roots of the words used to describe air. Just for fun, combine these parts of words to make the words above.

atmo = air

sphere = globe or ball

tropo = to turn

strato = cover or layer

meso = middle

thermo = hot or heated

ozo = smell

The Earth's Atmosphere Map

*Name:*_____

Scale

1" = 10 miles

Note: Earth not drawn to scale.

The Earth's Atmosphere Map
Teacher's Version

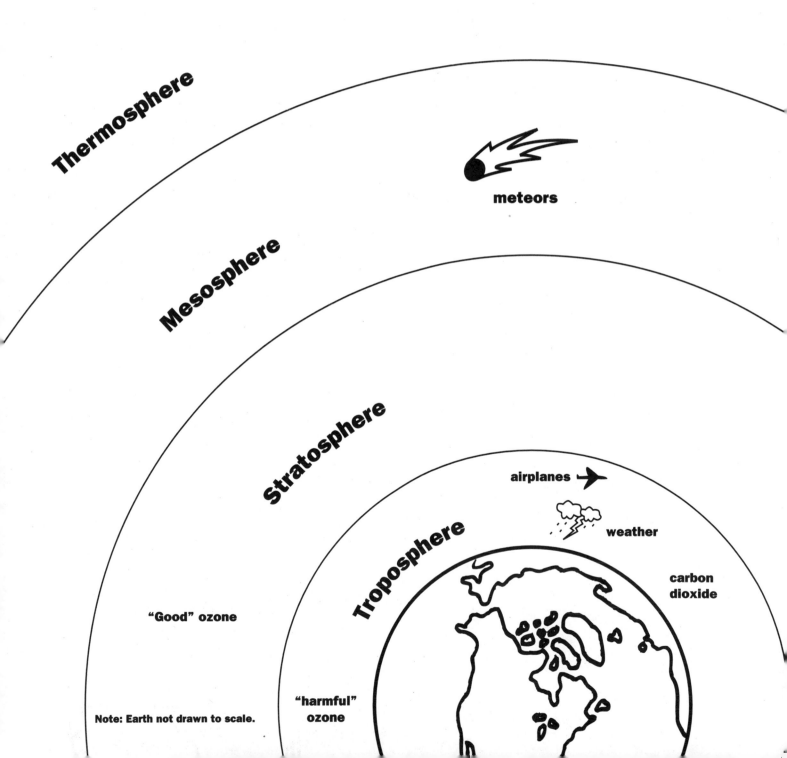

Scale

1" = 10 miles

Thermosphere

Mesosphere

meteors

Stratosphere

airplanes ➤

weather

Troposphere

carbon dioxide

"Good" ozone

"harmful" ozone

Note: Earth not drawn to scale.

Energy Conservation

The Challenge

Energy is power. If you have power, you can get out of bed in the morning, ride a bicycle and do your homework. You have energy, which you actually made by eating the right foods, drinking fresh water and keeping yourself healthy.

Energy is also the power that allows you to turn on the lights, heat the water to wash your face and ride the bus to school. That kind of energy comes from several different sources.

Most likely, the energy to heat your house, turn on your lights or get you to school comes from the burning of fossil fuels — oil, coal and natural gas. These energy sources are the remains of plants and animals that lived on this planet millions of years ago. They are called non-renewable energy because they can only be used once.

One of the best things about fossil fuels is that they're cheap to get and cheap to use. But when we use fossil fuels, we create pollution. We pollute water and the land when we remove the fuels from the earth. We also pollute the air with carbon dioxide and other toxins when we burn these fuels.

We can use nuclear reactions to create electricity, but we do have to dispose of radioactive waste, which is so powerful it can be deadly. We can also draw energy from the sun, as solar power. But, to make that kind of energy you need a lot of sunny days, and that's not always going to happen.

Energy can come from windmills, which capture the power in wind. It can come from hydroelectric dams, which use the force of water to make power. But dams can stop fish from moving up rivers. Solar, wind and hydro power are renewable sources, because they can be used over and over again.

Did You Know?

- Only 5 percent of the world's people live in the United States. But, Americans use 34 percent of the world's energy. We import (bring in from other countries) 70 percent of all the oil we use.
- If you live in North America, you use the equivalent of 22 barrels of oil per year. One barrel holds 42 gallons of oil.
- Recycling is an important way to conserve energy. Recycling aluminum into a new product saves 90 to 95 percent of the energy it would take to make the product from new aluminum.
- Nature has a great cooling system. Planting one shade tree can cool yards, gardens and buildings by 10° during the hottest part of the day, and can reduce energy consumption from 15 to 35 percent.

The Energy Conservation chapter of the *Animal Tracks Activity Guide* corresponds to the Polar Bear chapter of the *Animal Tracks* children's book.

1. Energy Sources

Subjects:
Science, Environmental Science, Social Science, Language Arts, Health

Process Skills:
Listening, reading, writing, grouping facts, conducting research

Grades:
4–6

Cognitive Task Level:
Average to difficult

Time for Activity:
30 minutes to start, then as a homework assignment

Key Vocabulary:
Chemical, jojoba, organic, fossil, nuclear, electricity, hydraulic, hydroelectric, petroleum, windmill, refuse

Intended Learning Outcomes:
Completing this activity will allow students to:
- Observe different types of energy sources
- Learn more about energy and where it comes from
- Conduct their own research reports on energy sources.

Background
Sources of energy are all around us, and come in a variety of different forms. Energy for a person is different than energy for an automobile. In this activity, the teacher demonstrates several different types of energy, and assigns a research report topic for small groups of students.

Materials
- Picture of the sun (optional)
- Fruit or vegetable
- Container of vegetable oil
- Piece of firewood
- Piece of charcoal or coal
- Container of motor oil
- Gas lighter
- Cup of water and an empty cup
- Child's pinwheel
- Picture of lightning or a light bulb
- Picture of a nuclear power plant
- Piece of discarded trash
- Battery

Procedure
1. Using the information on pages 78–79, demonstrate the different energy sources. Write the names of the different types of energy sources on the chalkboard.

2. Once students have received their introduction to energy sources, inform them that they will be conducting research reports to find out more about their energy sources. Break the class into groups of two or three students. Assign each group a different energy source. Instruct each group to complete a three-page report about the energy source. Since the project will be a collaborative effort between two or three students, encourage the students to divide the work, so that each student contributes a section to the final report.

3. Take a trip to the library. Work with the librarian to show the students how to find the information they need to complete the report on their energy source. Be sure they know how to use the encyclopedia and other resources. Provide time for the students to do their research, work together in their groups and write the report.

4. After the reports are completed, have each group give a five-minute presentation about the energy source they studied.

5. After all the presentations have been given, initiate a discussion with your class about what they learned. Ask your class to choose the safest energy source, the most efficient energy source, the energy source that's least destructive to the environment and the cheapest energy source. Then, write a list of the energy sources on the board, and have the class vote for the "best" source. You may have them vote for the top two or three.

Extensions/Modifications

- As a simpler version of this activity, assign the energy words as homework vocabulary assignments to your students. Have them complete sentences using the words.
- An even simpler version of the activity would be to simply conduct the demonstration as described in the activity.
- To extend this activity, have each student write a one-page essay on which three energy sources they would choose as the "best" sources of energy for the world. Tell them to explain why they chose what they did. This can be given as an in-class assignment or as a homework assignment. When the essays have been completed, ask some students to read theirs aloud. Display the completed essays in the classroom.

Energy Sources

Sunlight: Point to the sun, or hold up a picture of the sun. The light that comes to the earth from the sun is pure energy. The sun is the original energy source. Nearly all other sources of energy originally got their energy from the sun. Organic matter, like plants, convert solar energy into leaves, flowers and fruits. Animals, which eat organic matter, convert the energy into body mass. When animals die, their energy is decomposed and over extensive time, becomes stored as oil, coal or natural gas.

Food: Hold up an apple, orange or other fruit or vegetable. Food is the source of energy used by people. Food that we eat is digested, and the stored energy is used by the body to keep the heart beating, the blood pumping and the body growing. When a body has "low blood sugar," the body needs to eat and process more energy, so it can continue working, playing and growing.

Organic Oils: Hold up a bottle of vegetable oil. Vegetable oil and animal oil have played an important role in human history. Vegetable oils, like olive oil, corn oil or safflower oil, are often used in cooking. Jojoba oil (from the jojoba bean) is used in cooking or lubricating, as well as in lotions and soaps. Animal oil, like that from whales, seals and livestock, was used in the past for lighting lamps as well as for waterproofing.

Wood: Hold up a piece of firewood. Wood comes from trees, which are, of course, plants. The plants got their energy from the sun. When trees are cut down and burned, they release their energy in the form of heat. Many homes are heated with wood-burning stoves.

Fossil Fuels

The following three energy sources come from prehistoric fossils. Like the methods described above, ancient plants absorbed the energy from the sun and converted it into more plants. Ancient animals, like dinosaurs, ate the plants. When the plants and animals died, their remains collected under mountains of earth and, over millions of years, they decomposed into a source of fuel. The remains of these plants and animals are what we refer to as fossil fuels.

Coal: Hold up a piece of charcoal, or, if possible, a piece of real coal. Coal is burned to heat homes and run electrical machinery. About 20 percent of the energy we use comes from coal.

Oil: Hold up a container of motor oil (preferably in clear plastic so students can see the oil). Other petroleum products similar to motor oil are burned to fuel motor vehicles and heat homes. About 45 percent of energy used comes from oil.

Natural Gas: Hold up a lighter, and light it. Natural gas is used to heat the homes of many people. About 25 percent of the energy we use comes from natural gas. The fuel used in lighters is not the same as the natural gas used to heat homes, but the lighter can be used as an example.

Most of the energy used by people today comes from these fossil fuels. But fossil fuels are limited in their supply, can pollute and are sometimes hard to find.

Other Energy Sources

The following energy sources do not require the sun. They are derived from other aspects of the earth's ecosystem.

Water: Pour water from one cup to another, simulating a waterfall. Water is not an energy source, but water is used to generate energy. Water falling downhill is used to run turbines, which generate electricity. This is called hydroelectric power. About 5 percent of the world's power is now produced by hydro-electric dams. A similar type of energy comes from geothermal energy. Pockets of boiling water under the earth's surface send steam to the surface of the earth. This hot water also can be used to generate electricity. Dams can impede the movement of fish up and down river to reach spawning grounds or for other migratory purposes.

Wind: Hold up a pinwheel and blow on it. Winds that blow can be used to turn windmills, which generate electricity. Windmills have been used for centuries in some parts of the world, like Holland. Windmills are also used in the United States.

Electricity: Hold up a picture of lightning, and/or a light bulb. An electrical storm contains a great deal of natural electrical energy. Benjamin Franklin first proved that lightning was electricity in 1752. His discovery helped scientists learn how to harness electricity and how to generate electricity from other methods. The electricity we use today was created by other sources, not by the energy released by lightning.

Nuclear Power: Hold up a picture of a nuclear power plant. Nuclear power comes from the radioactive ore uranium. It produces far more power per ton than any other energy source. Nuclear power does not contribute to air pollution. However, radioactive waste is hazardous to living things. Exposure to radioactive materials can result in mutations, illness or death. The drawback to using nuclear power is finding a safe place to dispose of the nuclear waste. About 6 percent of the energy used in the world comes from nuclear power.

Refuse-derived fuel: Hold up a piece of discarded trash. Now, we are able to extract energy from garbage! Garbage is burned in a waste-to-energy facility. As it burns, water pipes are heated. This hot water is used to generate electricity. Most waste-to-energy facilities produce enough energy to run the plant and supply additional power to the community. This is a small but growing source of energy.

Chemical energy: Hold up a battery. Batteries create energy through chemical reactions. When different chemicals react with one another, energy is released. Eventually, the reaction stops, and the battery must be replaced. Batteries are used in motor vehicles and many smaller appliances, like clocks, hearing aids and toys.

2. Energy Activities
Background

Everything that occurs in the world comes about as an exchange of energy. But energy cannot be seen, heard, felt or touched. It is invisible, yet it's the force that makes life possible. Trying to explain energy can be very difficult. These simple activities allow children to observe the effects of energy. With some guidance, the students can develop their own explanations for how these events happened, and, in the process, gain greater understanding of the nature of energy.

Subjects:
Science, Environmental Science, Language Arts

Process Skills:
Hands-on manipulation, teamwork, verbal communication, following directions

Grades:
3–4

Cognitive Task Level:
Average

Time for Activity:
30 minutes

Key Vocabulary:
Gravity, force, electricity, solar, hydroelectric, windmill

Intended Learning Outcomes:
Completing this activity will allow students to:
- Conduct experiments to learn about how energy works in our world
- Observe changes that occur due to the forces of energy
- Work in groups to explain the phenomena they observe.

Materials

- ❑ Watch or clock with second hand
- ❑ 2 thermometers
- ❑ 6 tart pans, 3 inches in diameter (one pan painted black)
- ❑ Solar calculator
- ❑ Desk lamp
- ❑ Rock, about 4 inches high
- ❑ Flat board, about 1 foot by 18 inches long
- ❑ Toy car
- ❑ Newspaper
- ❑ 2 cups of ice
- ❑ Paper cut into 3-inch by 6-inch strips
- ❑ Paper cut into 3-inch by 2-inch squares (4 per experiment)
- ❑ Tape
- ❑ Unused pencil
- ❑ Paper
- ❑ Paper clips
- ❑ String
- ❑ Handout
  - *Energy Experiments*

Procedure

This activity is best conducted outdoors in an area protected from the wind.

1. After a discussion of energy and its various forms, direct your students in these energy experiments. Divide the class into two groups. Hand out the Energy Experiments worksheet.

2. Have one group perform the solar, cooling and heat experiments. Have the second group perform the gravity, physical, insulation and wind experiments. Hand out the necessary materials to each group.

You may want to instruct the groups to divide the activities so that one or two students conduct each experiment, or have the whole group go through each experiment together. Some experiments take longer than others. Have the students plan their time so that they can complete the experiments in the time allotted for the activity.

3. Be available to assist your students in their experiments or in their explanations of what happened. Guide them through difficult explanations.

4. When all the experiments are completed, take a few minutes and have your students explain the experiments to each other. Have each group explain to the others what experiments they conducted and how they worked. Be sure they clean up the remains of the experiments.

5. When everyone is back in their seats, use this period to test for knowledge. Randomly ask students about each of the different experiments. If they communicated well with each other, each student should know the answer, or be able to guess at the answer. If necessary, explain the concepts again at this time.

Extensions/Modifications
- To expand this activity or make it more difficult, look up more energy experiments in books and curricula.
- To simplify this activity, you may choose to conduct the experiments as part of a demonstration and discussion activity.

Energy Experiments

Name _____

- ❑ Watch or clock with second hand
- ❑ 2 thermometers
- ❑ 6 tart pans, 3 inches in diameter (one pan painted black)

- ❑ Water
- ❑ Solar calculator
- ❑ Desk lamp

Solar:

1. Solar energy creates electricity using solar cells. A solar calculator provides an example of this. Using the calculator, make a simple calculation. Then find the solar cells and cover them with your finger for 30 seconds. Keep your finger on the solar cells and try to make the calculation again. What happens? _____

   _____

   _____

   _____

2. Set out an unpainted aluminum pie tin and a second tin, painted with black paint. Fill both pans with exactly the same amount of water. After ten minutes, check the temperature of both pans. What are the differences? Why did this occur? _____

   _____

   _____

   _____

Cooling:

3. Place one aluminum pan with water in it in the sun. Place another under a shady tree. After ten minutes, check the temperatures of the water in the pans. Which is warmer? Why?_____

   _____

   _____

   _____

Heat:

4. Place a desk lamp over an aluminum pan with water in it. Set a second one, with the same amount of water, away from the lamp. After ten minutes, check the temperature of each. Which is warmer? Why? _____

   _____

   _____

   _____

Energy Experiments (Continued)

Materials
- ❏ Rock, about 4 inches high
- ❏ Newspaper
- ❏ Flat board, about 1 foot by 18 inches long
- ❏ 2 cups of ice
- ❏ Toy car

Gravity:
1. Place a board over a rock so one end is higher than the other. Place a toy car on the incline. What happens? Why? Try placing the board flat. Does the car move? Why not? _____

_____

_____

Physical:
2. Place a rock on the ground. What happens? Now place your hand behind the rock and push gently. The rock moves. What makes the rock move? _____

_____

_____

Insulation:
3. Place a cup filled with ice in the sun. Wrap newspaper around a second cup of ice, and place it in the sun. The ice in which cup melts faster? Why? _____

_____

_____

Materials
- ❏ Paper cut into 3-inch by 6-inch strips
- ❏ Paper cut into 3-inch by 2-inch squares (4 per experiment)
- ❏ Tape
- ❏ Unused pencil
- ❏ Paper
- ❏ Paper clips
- ❏ String

Wind:
1. Wrap the large piece of paper around the pencil. Tape it. Make sure it fits loosely. Tape the four squares to the paper. Tie the paper clip to the string and tape the other end of the string to the paper tube. Blow on the blades of paper. You have created a windmill! The wind from your blowing on it should cause the tube to turn, and it should wind the string with the paper clip up the tube. Why does the windmill turn? _____

_____

This works best with slightly heavy paper—like construction paper or used brochures.

These are the blades.

Hold pencil here.

Blow on blades.

Blow on blades to pull string around and pull up paper clip.

3. Energy and Society

Subjects:
Social Studies, Health, Language Arts

Process Skills:
Reading, searching for key words, analyzing, verbal communication

Grades:
2–6

Cognitive Task Level:
Simple

Time for Activity:
5 to 10 minutes per day for duration of unit

Key Vocabulary:
Articles, efficiency, energy, references, sources

Intended Learning Outcomes:
Completing this activity will allow students to:
- Participate in creating an energy bulletin board
- Find articles and pictures relating to energy in society
- Learn about different sources of energy and energy concerns
- Share what they have learned with classmates.

Background

Energy is such an integral part of everyday life that we often overlook it. References to energy occur everywhere: the energy bill that arrives each month, newspaper reports about oil spills and catalogs that sell energy-efficient products.

This activity encourages students to look for and bring in articles, pictures, flyers and other references to energy. Students put them on a large bulletin board. Each day, as additions come in, students will learn and share their knowledge about energy with each other.

Materials
- ☐ Large bulletin board space, about 3 feet by 3 feet
- ☐ Pins or staples

Procedure

1. Make room on a bulletin board for this activity by removing all other items. If possible, make a sign that explains the purpose of the bulletin board, like "Energy Board," "We Learn About Energy" or another slogan.

2. Instruct your students to look in magazines, newspapers, catalogs and other written sources for articles, pictures, advertisements and references to energy or energy problems. They can bring in articles that relate to energy shortages, energy solutions, energy sources, energy costs, energy refunds or savings or any other aspect of energy they find.

3. You may choose to divide the bulletin board into sections, including "Energy Concerns," "Energy Solutions" or "Energy and Politics."

4. Require each student to bring in a minimum of two energy references (more if appropriate). At the start of the activity each day, have the students who brought references stand up and explain the article briefly to the class. Then have the student pin the article on the bulletin board. If the bulletin board is divided into sections, ask where the article should be placed.

Extensions/Modifications

- To expand this activity, you may choose to add a writing assignment with each article. This assignment would require the student to write down the source of the article and include a brief description of the purpose of the article.
- Your bulletin board will be filled with references to energy from a variety of different sources. You may take a picture of it, or move the entire bulletin board from class to class, sharing what your class has learned with others.
- Instead of a bulletin board, you may choose to make flashcards of some pictures of energy sources. Then quiz your students on how well they identify the pictures and explain how the energy sources work.

4. How Much Energy Do You Use?

Subjects:
Science, Math, Social Studies, Home Economics

Process Skills:
Counting, multiplication, use of calculators, comparing, data gathering

Grades:
3–6

Cognitive Task Level:
Average to difficult

Time for Activity:
15 minutes preparation, one day's homework, 20 minutes classwork

Intended Learning Outcomes:
Completing this activity will allow students to:
- Observe the items that use energy in their own homes
- Calculate the energy cost for their own homes
- Compare this cost with others in their class and with the national average.

Background

U. S. residents use more energy now than we ever have in the past. There are many reasons for this. As more people populate the country, energy needs rise. Technology advances, such as industrial processes, sophisticated machinery and computers also require increased energy. Our everyday lives are filled with electrical appliances that our grandparents never used.

Why is our energy bill so high? This activity gives your students a chance to work on some real-life math problems. This activity bases its numbers on cost figures from one utility. Energy figures in your area may be different. Your local energy utility can give you figures that show the average expenditure per household in your community.

Materials
- ❑ Calculators
- ❑ Handout
  - *Energy Home Survey* worksheet

Procedure

1. Start by asking your students if they ever heard their parents complain about the cost of energy. Explain that the monthly utility bill is directly related to the amount of energy the household uses, and that this activity will help them find the "energy-eaters" in the house.

2. Distribute the Energy Home Survey worksheet and assign the homework.

3. When students have completed the homework assignment, assist them in answering the questions and completing the math.

4. Ask them if they found appliances in their homes they think they could live without, such as an electric can opener or an electric plate warmer.

Extensions/Modifications
- A good introduction to this activity is to encourage students to ask a grandparent, or older relative or neighbor about what life was like when they were children. Many grandparents grew up before television, commuter flights and digital clocks. The student could interview the senior and write a report comparing an aspect of energy use "then" vs. "now."

Energy Home Survey

Name _____

Do this survey twice: once in the morning before school, and once just before dinner. It will help you determine how much energy you use.

Appliance Electrical Appliances	Multiply by	Subtotal	Total per day
Incandescent Lights: Number of lights on =	1¢ per hour		
Fluorescent lights: Number of lights on =	1¢ per every 4 hours		
Television: Number of sets on =	4¢ per hour		
Radio: Number of sets on =	1¢ per hour		
Stereo: Number of sets on =	2¢ per hour		
Microwave oven: Number of ovens on =	15¢ per hour		
Computer: Number of computers on =	1¢ per hour		
Vacuum cleaner: Number on =	9¢ per hour		
Portable heater: Number on =	15¢ per hour		
Air conditioner: Number on =	55¢ per hour		
Total for all subtotal usage			
Total usage in one day			

Add up all the numbers in the Subtotal column. This subtotal is the total cost for these appliances in one hour.

Some of these appliances will be on for more than one hour, some less. Based on what you know about your household, write the total number of hours and the total cost in one day for these appliances in the Total per day columns above.

(Example 1: If two stereos are on for eight hours a day, you multiply 2 (stereos) x 2¢ per hour x 8 hours = 32¢ per day. Example 2: If you vacuum for 1/2 hour, multiply by 9¢ per hour x .5 hours = 4.5 ¢ per day.

Energy Home Survey (Continued)

Periodic Appliances

Some items are not used all the time. They create a cost only when they are used.

Periodic Appliances Appliance and loads per month	Multiply by	Total per month
Dishwasher:		
Loads =	10¢ per load	
Washing machine:		
Loads =	5¢ per load	
Electric clothes dryer:		
Loads =	67¢ per load	
Gas clothes dryer:		
Loads =	16¢ per load	
Total usage for one month		

These answers give you the total cost per month, based on how much your family uses these appliances.

Periodic Appliances Appliance and average use per month	Total per month
Gas water heater:	$13.00
Electric water heater:	$45.00
Refrigerator:	$16.00
Extra freezer:	$18.00
Electric heating system:	
Small home	$85.00
Large home	$250.00
Gas heating system:	
Small home	$28.00
Large home	$120.00
	Total usage for one month

With your teacher's help, try to figure out your home energy costs for one month. Compare it to the bill that your parents receive each month. How do they compare?

My estimate _____

My parent's bill _____

Did your estimate come close to the actual cost? If not, why do you think they differ? _____

_____

_____

_____

_____

5. Changing Habits — An Energy Self-Audit

Background

When people make changes in their own lives, they feel the excitement of their accomplishments and share that excitement with others. Now that your students are experts about energy use in their homes, encourage them to come up with ways they can reduce energy use and conserve natural resources in the own lives.

Subjects:
Social Studies, Home Economics, Health, Language Arts

Process Skills:
Decision-making, self-observation, inventing solutions

Grades:
3–6

Cognitive Task Level:
Average

Time for Activity:
20 minutes

Key Vocabulary:
Habits, decisions

Intended Learning Outcomes:
Completing this activity will allow students to:

- Observe their own habits of energy consumption
- Make decisions about habits they wish to change
- Feel they are making a positive change toward conserving energy and natural resources.

The Changing Energy Habits worksheet provides many ideas for students to change energy-wasting habits. Try to come up with a few more with your class. Encourage your students to think of at least five actions they can take to conserve energy. If a student feels he or she cannot make the changes, discuss the reasons why, and respect their limitations. This activity is intended to reward and encourage, not condemn or place demands upon students.

Materials

❑ Handout
  - *Changing Energy Habits*

Procedure

1. To help your students learn energy conservation, tell them it's their turn to put the knowledge they gained from their energy audit (Activity 4) to good use.

2. Hand out the Changing Energy Habits worksheet and go over the options with them. Help them think of new ideas to reduce energy waste. Have them write their ideas on the space provided at the end of the worksheet.

3. Give your students ten minutes to go through their worksheets and make decisions about what actions they will take and what habits they will change.

4. After everyone has made their selections, ask several students what they are choosing to do. Ask them to explain why they choose these changes and how they plan to carry them out. Ask them how they expect their families to react to the changes.

5. Have your students keep their worksheets in their desks. After a week or two, have your students write a one-page essay on the changes they made and why. Have them include the effect these changes have had on the family. Has there been a reduction in the energy bill? Has it affected the way the family acts, thinks or interacts? Ask students to talk about what happened when they changed their behavior. Ask them if they feel they took steps to save energy and natural resources.

Extensions/Modifications

- To expand this lesson, take the numbers listed for energy usage in the How Much Energy Do You Use lesson, and calculate how much energy has been saved by such changes. For example, if a student switches from an incandescent light to a fluorescent bulb, have him/her calculate the savings.
- Take part in an energy audit at school. Have your class encourage the school to start recycling and reusing paper, turn off the lights during recess and after school, use reusable cups, bring reusable thermoses and lunch bags to school or install water dams in the school toilets, etc. The students will feel empowered by their accomplishments and the school will save money.
- For ESL students, the worksheet can be easily translated into other languages. Encourage these students to share energy-saving actions from their own cultures.

Changing Energy Habits

Pledge:

I pledge to make changes in my life to reduce the waste of energy and natural resources. I will select at least five of the following suggestions and start saving energy today!

Place a check mark next to the five actions you will take to conserve energy and save natural resources:

____ Switch from disposable batteries to reusable batteries

____ Encourage my parents to have regular car tune-ups for energy efficiency

____ Make sure my parents recycle used motor oil

____ Use both sides of a sheet of paper before throwing it out

____ Use smaller sheets of paper when I write notes

____ Suggest we get a clean-erase board to reduce paper waste

____ Switch from electric clock to battery-operated clock

____ Recycle paper when it has been used

____ Turn off lights when leaving a room

____ Turn off water while brushing teeth

____ Walk or ride a bike to the store or to school whenever I can

____ Trade books, toys, etc. with a friend, or donate them to Goodwill instead of throwing them away

____ Compost garbage

____ Use cloth napkins at school and home to save paper

____ Use reusable cups instead of disposable ones

____ Use a hand-held can opener instead of an electric one

____ Use a solar-operated calculator instead of a battery-operated one

____ Wear a solar-powered watch

____ Air-dry my hair instead of blowing it dry

____ Place a timer in the shower and encourage everyone in the family to take shorter showers

____ Take five-minute showers

____ Put on a sweater and socks when I'm cold instead of turning up the heat

____ Suggest to my family that we keep the thermostat at 68 degrees

____ Ask my family to run the washers and dryers at night, when there is less demand for energy

____ Close the drapes in the summer to keep the cool air inside

____ Ask my parents to purchase a water heater insulator

____ Ask my parents to turn down the heat on the water heater from high to medium

____ Install toilet dams or place bottles of water into my toilets to conserve water

____ Recycle aluminum cans, glass bottles, plastic bottles and newspapers

____ Open the refrigerator only long enough to get what I need, and not stand in front of the open door deciding what to eat

____ Take part in a school-wide effort to save energy and natural resources at school

____ Use a hand-powered lawnmower instead of a motor-powered lawnmower

____ Replace my electric pencil sharpener with a hand-held one

____ Turn the radio, stereo and television off when I leave the room

____ Avoid using portable heaters, if possible

____ Avoid running the dishwasher unless it is full

____ Other things I will do: _____

_____

_____

_____

_____

I pledge to make these changes and help save energy and natural resources for the future!

Resources for Energy Conservation

Books for Students

* *Fuel Resources*, by A.S. Brown. Franklin Watts. A children's science book that describes energy and the most common sources of fuel in the world today. Pictures and diagrams illustrate the concepts.

* *Technology: Science At Work*, by Robin McKie. Franklin Watts. Chapters touch on electricity, computers, space, manufacturing and other aspects of technology. Pictures and diagrams help illustrate the concepts.

Video and Audio

* *Solar Energy: How It Works* (video), by Churchill Film.

* *This World of Energy: II* (filmstrip), by National Geographic Society.

* *The Banana Slug String Band* (audio tapes and songbooks). Available from PO Box 717, Pescadero, CA 94060; 408-429-9806.

Books for Adults

* *Two Minutes A Day For A Greener Planet*, by Marjorie Lamb. Harper and Row. Hundreds of ideas for ways to save energy and natural resources, many of which are appropriate for kids, too.

* *The Environmental Address Book*, by Michael Levine Perigee. Includes addresses of the players in environmental issues, both the champions and the offenders.

Curricula

* *Living Lightly In The City*, by National Audubon Society. Available from 613 Riversville Road, Greenwich, CT 08630; 203-364-0520.

Recycling Paper & Aluminum

The Challenge

Look at an aluminum can next time you drink from one. In the United States, we use more than 80 billion aluminum cans each year. But the can you're holding might be made from recycled materials. To recycle something means you reuse it as it is, or you turn it into something else to use.

More than 60 percent of all those cans were recycled at least once. If we keep it up, all our aluminum cans will be made from cans we threw away!

Now, look at all the paper you use in a day. Your cereal might come in a paper box. Your toilet paper is paper. Your comic books and school books are paper. We throw away so much paper that it takes up 40 percent of all the space in our landfills. A landfill is the big garbage dump your trash goes to when you throw it "out."

If we recycle more paper and aluminum, we can help ourselves and nature. When we make paper and aluminum from new materials, we use up those natural resources, destroy habitats (when we cut down trees and mine for ore to make aluminum) and pollute our air and water. Recycling saves!

The Recycling Paper & Aluminum chapter of the *Animal Tracks Activity Guide* corresponds to the Raccoon chapter of the *Animal Tracks* children's book.

Did You Know?

- There are more than 6,000 landfills in the United States. Some rise 500 feet in the air, as tall as Washington, D.C.'s tallest building.
- Newspapers and telephone books are the most common items in landfills. It takes 50,000 trees to make our Sunday newspapers. If we recycle 10 percent of all our newspapers, we can save 25 million trees.
- Each American uses 600 pounds of paper, the weight of a tiger, annually. We throw away enough paper each year to build a 12-foot high wall from Los Angeles to New York.
- Aluminum comes from bauxite, a non-renewable ore.
- Making one new aluminum can takes as much energy as making 20 recycled ones. Recycled aluminum products means we don't use 90 percent of the energy we did to make a new one. And, we save 95 percent of pollution that would have gone into the air.

1. What is Packaging Really Made From?

Subjects:
Science, Language Arts, Social Studies, Environmental Studies

Process Skills:
Naming, comparing, touching, describing, identifying

Grades:
3–4

Cognitive Task Level:
Simple to average

Time for Activity:
30 minutes

Key Vocabulary:
Natural resources, petroleum, ore, bauxite, organic, packaging

Intended Learning Outcomes:
Completing this activity will allow students to:
- Learn what natural resources are and where they come from
- Identify and name the most common materials used in packaging
- Name the natural resources used to make packaging.

Background

About 30 percent of all the plastics we use are packaging. This includes beverage containers, food wrappers and product labels. We need some packaging to preserve the freshness of the product, to make it easy to transport, to prevent spoiling or tampering and to advertise the product. However, over-packaging wastes natural resources and increases the cost of the product. For students to understand that recycling saves natural resources, they need to learn that packages are made from valuable resources. Recycling puts these resources back into the packaging market again instead of sending them to the landfill.

Materials
Products made from:
- ❏ Aluminum (aluminum can)
- ❏ Steel and tin (soup can)
- ❏ Plastic (beverage bottle)
- ❏ Glass (beverage or food container)
- ❏ Paper (packaging, paper bag, etc.)
- ❏ Organic (orange with peel, banana and peel, peanuts in the shell, etc.)
- ❏ Mixed materials (juice box, disposable diaper, milk carton)
- ❏ Magnet
- ❏ Chalkboard
- ❏ Handout
  - *What is Packaging?*

Procedure

1. Explain to students that much of what we throw into the landfill is packaging. But what is packaging? And why do we need packaging? Ask your class to come up with reasons why packaging is important. Use the Background as your guide. Write some of these reasons on the chalkboard under the heading, "Why We Need Packaging."

2. Distribute the *What is packaging?* worksheet. Bring out the examples of packaging. Hold up each item and ask what materials are used to make the item. You may want to write the names of the materials on the board. Have the student fill out their worksheets.

3. Describe what natural resources were used to make those materials. See the teacher's version of the *What is packaging?* worksheet for a list of the correct answers. You may also wish to write these natural resources on the board.

4. Finally, pass the items around the class. Have them touch the items and describe their physical characteristics (such as smooth, cool, dry, wet or crinkly). Select a few students to help you. Try the magnet on all the items. Only the steel can is magnetic.

5. Ask the class to describe any other observations they may have about these items and where they come from.

6. Start a discussion by asking if your students have ever seen an over-packaged product or non-recyclable packaging. Explain that when an item is not recycled, it goes to the landfill and is never used again. But, when an item is recycled, the natural resource is used again, reducing the need for more natural resources. Therefore, recycling saves natural resources.

Extensions/Modifications

- For younger students, do not use the handout. Just describe the different items as part of a discussion.
- For younger students or for ESL students, assign the materials and natural resources as vocabulary words. Then have them write sentences spelling the words correctly and using them correctly in context. (Example: "My screen door is made from aluminum, which is made from bauxite ore." Or, "The plastic watering can my mom uses is made from petroleum.")
- For advanced students, assign a report as homework. Have students look up one of the natural resources used in packaging and write a one-page report about that resource.

What is Packaging?
Teacher's Version
Answers to the questions on the student handout.

Item		Material	Natural resources	Suggested description
1.	Can	Aluminum	Bauxite ore	smooth, shiny
2.	Can	Steel or tin	Iron ore and tin	smooth, gray
3.	Bottle	Plastic	Petroleum	clear, flexible
4.	Bottle	Glass	Sand, soda ash, limestone	clear, cool, smooth
5.	An old test	Paper	Trees	dry, white, crinkly
6.	Food and yard waste or compost	Plants	Plants	smelly, soft, damp
7.	Mixed materials			
	Juice box	Paper, petroleum, metal		
	Disposable diaper	Paper, plastic		
	Milk carton	Paper, plastic		

What is Packaging?

Name _____

As your teacher holds up each item, fill in the blanks below:

Item	What material is it made from?	What natural resource is it made from?	What does it feel like?
Example:			
Can	*Aluminum*	*Bauxite*	*smooth, shiny, cool*

2. Cash for Trash

Background

We use more than 80 billion aluminum cans each year. About 60 percent of today's aluminum cans are made from recycled aluminum. Aluminum cans have a high recycling value because recycling aluminum is much cheaper and requires less energy than manufacturing products from virgin bauxite ore, the raw natural resource used in the manufacture of aluminum.

Subjects:
Language Arts, Social Studies, Economics, Art

Process Skills:
Planning, decision-making, cooperative work, community involvement, computation, communication

Grades:
3–6

Cognitive Task Level:
Average

Time for Activity:
Varies

Key Vocabulary:
Recycling center, aluminum, bauxite, fund-raiser

Intended Learning Outcomes:
Completing this activity will allow students to:
- Plan and execute a fund-raising activity for a cause of their choice
- Write a financial plan and track the financial progress of the project
- Develop community involvement and communications skills.

Aluminum cans are valuable beverage containers to recycle in the United States. Most towns in the United States have recycling centers where aluminum cans can be turned in for cash. This makes recycling aluminum cans an excellent choice for fund-raising endeavors. On average, 26 cans make one pound of aluminum.

Materials
- ☐ Bags or boxes for collecting cans
- ☐ Storage area
- ☐ Class calendar
- ☐ Poster boards, markers and tacks for signs
- ☐ Handout
  - *Cash for Trash Fund-raiser Form*

Procedure

1. Before starting the fund-raiser, ask the principal and custodian if aluminum cans may be stored at the school site. Use the *Cash for Trash Fund-raiser Form* to find out other necessary information about starting a recycling fund-raiser. Have your students conduct as much of the work as possible.

2. Ask your class to choose a cause for which they would like to earn money. You may want to provide them with some options. Is your community trying to raise money for a new hospital? Perhaps you want to earn money to buy something for the school, or to donate funds to an environmental organization to support conservation efforts.

3. Use the *Cash for Trash Fund-raiser Form* to divide the duties. One group of students can find out about the best recycling center for the program. The Public Relations Group must make posters and flyers and distribute them. They may also design a

Public Service Announcement (PSA). (See the Madison Avenue activity in this unit.) The Project Managers must be responsible for an organized event on the day of the drive.

4. Establish a bookkeeping system that your students can help maintain. Or maintain it yourself and use the funds generated for math problems with your students.

5. When you have achieved your fundraising goals, be sure to let the community know, using PSAs. Follow up with letters thanking the community for their support.

Extensions/Modifications
- Fund-raising events can be executed in several ways. You may choose to have a one-day event at the school site on a Saturday morning. You may also be able to have the fund-raiser at the local recycling center, with the proceeds from all aluminum recycling for one day going to the class project. Students can be assigned roles — assisting in unloading cars, crushing cans or placing cans in storage bags. If different grades or classes are competing for the number of pounds they collect, borrow a large scale and supervise older students who can watch the scale and record the donations correctly for each grade or class.
- You can also develop an on-going recycling program at a recycling center. The recycling center keeps track of the pounds of aluminum specifically donated to the school. Once a month, the center sends a check to the school for the aluminum donated in the school's name.

Cash for Trash Fund-raiser Form
Teacher's section

Aluminum Recycling project to raise funds for:

_____ Time line for project (Set a date for the completion of each requirement)
_____ Receive approval from principal

Public Relations Group

Names of students who will complete these tasks _____

_____

_____ Ask local businesses if they will post a flyer or poster about the fund-raiser
_____ Make posters for posting in stores
_____ Makc flyers to send home
_____ Design a Public Service Announcement (PSA)

Recycling Center Information

Names of students who will complete these tasks _____

_____

_____ What is the closest facility for our purposes?
_____ Will they pick up materials at the school site?
_____ How much do they pay per pound of aluminum?
_____ Do they also take aluminum foil or scrap aluminum?
_____ Do they have a bookkeeping system there to keep track of our account?
_____ Would they be willing to host a recycling fund-raiser at their site on a Saturday morning if students volunteer to help?

Project Managers

Names of students who will complete these tasks _____

_____

_____ Create a sign-up list for students to assist at the recycling event
_____ Help unload cars
_____ Crush cans
_____ Clean up — place empty bags in garbage, separate other recyclable items that come in with the cans, etc.
_____ Assist at the scale
_____ Keep track of the pounds of aluminum and the dollar value

3. The Trash Creature
Background

The raccoon ("mascot" of this chapter in the student book, *Animal Tracks*) is always exploring new places. It touches items with its sensitive paws to identify them and find out if they're useful. Raccoons often find uses in things that people throw away. Creative reuse is a constructive way to help the environment. Artists and sculptors throughout the world are famous for finding new uses for cast-off items.

Subjects:
Art, Biology, Geography

Process Skills:
Hands-on manipulation, visualizing, planning, writing, creative thinking

Grades:
3–6

Cognitive Task Level:
Simple

Time for Activity:
One or two 50-minute class periods

Key Vocabulary:
Create, creature, continent, habitat, reuse

Intended Learning Outcomes:
Completing this activity will allow students to:
- Gain an appreciation of the "hidden value" of old or discarded items
- Develop their creative skills
- Consider animal needs and habitats.

By offering your students this fun activity, you are encouraging their natural creativity and setting a good example for reuse. As your students think of natural history information about their "trash creatures," they learn about other animals. If they need help thinking of ideas, have a few animal books or field guides available for them.

Materials (Suggestions to inspire creativity)
- ❑ Paper clips
- ❑ Broken objects (except for broken glass)
- ❑ Pieces of packages
- ❑ Bottle tops
- ❑ Foil balls
- ❑ Rubber bands
- ❑ Strapping materials
- ❑ Packing peanuts
- ❑ Polystyrene meat trays
- ❑ Pieces of string
- ❑ Fabric scraps
- ❑ Glue, stapler, paints, glitter
- ❑ Handout
  - *Trash creature description card*

Procedure

1. Tell your students to find items at home that have been discarded but which may still be useful in works of art or sculpture. Discuss with them the types of things to look for, such as those listed in the Materials section. Tell your students to be sure the items are clean. If you have access to a center that collects cast-off items, you may want to bring some things to class yourself.

2. When your students have brought their items in to class, have them create a "trash creature."

They can create any type of animal they wish, either real or fantasy, and they can decorate their trash creature with paints, glitter etc.

3. Cut the *Trash creature description card* so each student gets one. Have the students fill out the *Trash creature description card*. They must answer all the questions about their creature. If they need help thinking of ideas, have a few animal books or field guides available for them.

4. Create an art shelf in the classroom to display the finished trash creatures with their description cards. Invite other classes in. Have your students explain why they made their art using items that would otherwise have been thrown away, and how they thought up the information about their trash creatures.

Extensions/Modifications
- You may choose to do this activity after a visit to the zoo.
- For a simpler version of this activity, bring in polystyrene molds of shapes or animals from the hobby store. Let your students decorate the shapes with discarded materials or use them as the basis from which to add and build.
- More advanced students should first draw their art design on paper before they make it.
- Have your class work together on a life-sized trash creature. Poke holes in the bottom of aluminum cans and string them together to make legs or antennae. See how big an animal you can make.

Trash creature description card

Name of Student _____

Name of Creature _____

In what part of the world is this creature found? _____

What type of habitat does it prefer? _____

What does it eat? _____

Interesting facts about this animal _____

CUT HERE --

Trash creature description card

Name of Student _____

Name of Creature _____

In what part of the world is this creature found? _____

What type of habitat does it prefer? _____

What does it eat? _____

Interesting facts about this animal _____

CUT HERE --

Trash creature description card

Name of Student _____

Name of Creature _____

In what part of the world is this creature found? _____

What type of habitat does it prefer? _____

What does it eat? _____

Interesting facts about this animal _____

4. Madison Avenue

Subjects:
Language Arts, Creative Writing, Art, Economics

Process Skills:
Forming models, gathering data, defining goals, testing outcomes, writing, public speaking, hands-on art, teamwork

Grades:
4–6

Cognitive Task Level:
Average to difficult

Time for Activity:
Three to five class periods

Key Vocabulary:
Ad campaign, commercial, jingle, media, storyboard

Intended Learning Outcomes:
Completing this activity will allow students to:
- Design a media campaign to encourage consumers to buy products made from recycled materials
- Identify problems and offer solutions
- Consider career possibilities in art and advertising
- Create their own message using art and verbal skills.

Background

Advertising, with its high-tech component, is a multi-billion dollar business. To receive the same level of public attention as companies that sell products from non-recycled goods, recycling advocates have joined the media campaign. Their message is different. They inform the public that buying products made from recycled materials conserves natural resources and landfill space and reduces waste and pollution. Research has shown that consumers respond to bright, positive colorful ads that grab and hold attention.

In this lesson, students use their creativity to encourage consumers to buy recycled products. If possible, use a video camera to videotape the presentations so your students can see themselves in action.

Materials

- ❑ Poster boards (one or more per group)
- ❑ Felt pens and other art supplies
- ❑ Notebooks and scratch paper
- ❑ Books and magazines (used) for gathering ideas and information
- ❑ Computer graphics programs, if available
- ❑ Video camera (optional)

Procedure

1. Start a discussion with your students about advertising. Ask them about their favorite ads on television, in newspapers and magazines and on the radio. Ask them if any students have seen ads encouraging people to buy recycled products or to reuse items instead of throwing them away. Ask them what qualities they think make a good ad. Write these qualities on the board and have them write them down at their desks.

2. Inform your students that they will design an ad campaign to encourage consumers to do their part to reduce waste. Some possible themes:

- Encourage people to recycle at home

- Encourage consumers to buy recycled or recyclable products

- Encourage people to reuse items as much as possible

- Encourage people to buy a particular product because it is recycled or recyclable.

You and your students may come up with other ideas as well.

3. Divide your class into groups of three to six students. Have them name their organization and identify the theme of their ad campaign. Have your students write these on the same piece of paper on which they wrote the qualities of a good media campaign. Check to be sure each group has completed the above tasks. Provide time for them to scan magazines in class for ideas on how to present their message. As a homework assignment, have them watch television for ideas for commercials.

4. In class the following day, divide your class into their groups and distribute the poster boards and art materials. On the board, write down what the students must complete:

- Write a 15- to 30-second message and select someone to speak during the commercial.

- Design and create storyboard(s) that reinforce the spoken message during the commercial. During the commercial, the speaker must give the name of the organization, then speak the written message, while the other students hold up the storyboards. They may trade tasks during the commercial if they wish. The message can be in the form of a song or jingle, a poem or a statement. Encourage your students to be creative. It may take more than one class period to complete both the written and art aspects of the assignment. They will need time to rehearse their commercials, too. Give the students as much time as you think appropriate.

5. When all the groups have completed their assignment, set up the video camera. You can invite parents or other classes to attend. Have your students present their commercials. After each commercial, ask the other students their perceptions of the commercial's theme. See if the commercial succeeded in accomplishing its intended goal.

Extensions/Modifications

- For younger students, you may want to choose a particular theme for the students, and offer more help in coming up with ideas on how to present the theme. They may need more guidance and attention than older students.
- Younger students could also work individually to complete a picture or poster. These can be displayed downtown in a store that sells recycled products, or at the local recycling center.
- Older students can use video cameras to videotape their own commercials. Show the commercials to the rest of the class. See if the local television station will broadcast them as a Public Service Announcement.
- If your school has good computer graphics programs, allow students to use these in the creation of their storyboards.

Resources for Recycling Paper and Aluminum
Resources for Students

- *Aluminum Recycling: Your Next Assignment (video)*, by Aluminum Recycling Association. This 30-minute video is one of the best ever on recycling, with an emphasis on aluminum recycling.
- *Paper by Kids*, by Arnold Grummer, E. Dillon Press. A good book about making recycled paper.

- *How Paper Is Made*, by Lesley Perrins, Facts on File Press. Goes inside a paper-making plant to learn about the steps involved in making paper from trees.
- *The Incredible Paper Making Kit*, by T.G.I. Games, Inc. (8-2227 Queen Street, Bellingham, WA 98226). Contains two paper making screens and instructions for making paper.

Resources for Adults
- *Rubbish: The Archeology of Garbage*, by William Rathje. Published by Harper Collins. This book is written by the recognized national expert on solid waste in the United States.

Organizations
- *The Aluminum Association.*, 900 19th St., NW, Washington, DC 20006. They have written materials, videos, and education materials about aluminum recycling, most of which are free.
- *American Paper Institute*, 1250 Connecticut Avenue, NW, Suite 210, Washington, DC 20036; 202-463-2420.
- *The Mail Preference Service*, Direct Marketing Association, 11 West 42nd St. PO Box 3861, New York, NY 10163-3861. To reduce unwanted mail, request that your name be dropped from mailing list companies.

Recycling Plastics & Glass

The Challenge

To make plastics and glass, we use natural resources and lots of energy. We have to start with raw materials. Glass actually starts in the ground. First, we mine silica sand, soda ash and limestone. Then, we combine and heat them to such a high temperature that they melt. Finally, glass-makers form the mixture into jars, bottles, sheets and other shapes.

Creating new glass takes a toll on the environment. Mining can destroy land, ruining habitat for wildlife.

Mining also uses chemicals during the process of removing elements from the earth. These chemicals add to pollution. It also takes an amazing amount of energy to melt the raw materials to such high temperatures.

Plastics also are made from natural resources. Most plastic is made from water and petroleum, a fossil fuel formed millions of years ago. The reserves of petroleum in our earth today are all that we have left. We don't know how to make new petroleum. We create plastics in many shapes, using heat and pressure. The result can be clear or colored, and soft or hard.

When we're done using whatever came in glass or plastic containers, we either recycle the containers or toss them out. If we toss them, we throw them away forever. Plastics and glass do not break down, or disintegrate. But, if we recycle, we save valuable landfill space.

Did You Know?

- People—not nature—make plastic. We can recycle many plastics but we must be careful that we sort the varieties.
- Plastics can be deadly to marine and aquatic life. Plastic bags look like jellyfish, which sea turtles love to eat. Sea turtles mistake the bags for food and choke on them.
- The glass that's made from recycled glass creates 20 percent less air pollution and only half the water pollution that making new glass creates.

The Recycling Plastics & Glass chapter of the *Animal Tracks Activity Guide* corresponds to the Fox chapter of the *Animal Tracks* children's book.

1. Weight and Volume

Subjects:
Math, Science, Language Arts

Process Skills:
Use of calculators, use of scale, use of percentages, counting, recording, making bar graphs, analyzing results, working in groups

Grades:
3–6

Cognitive Task Level:
Average to difficult

Time for Activity:
50-minute classroom period

Key Vocabulary:
Weight, volume, percentage, landfill

Intended Learning Outcomes:
Completing this activity will allow students to:
- See how weight and volume impact landfill problems in very different ways
- Practice simple math skills in a real-life science activity
- Gain an understanding of the amount of waste produced by each person in one day.

Background

When concern over landfill space first became a national issue, few people knew what the inside of a landfill actually looked like. Wild speculations were made, like "Plastics compose 90 percent of our solid waste!" or "Organic waste biodegrades in landfills!" Some of these misconceptions linger to this day.

Bill Rathje, Ph.D., is an archaeologist and the founder of The Garbage Project, a research organization based in Tucson, Arizona. Dr Rathje and his students used the only method possible to find out what really fills up our landfills — by looking at it, measuring it, weighing it and counting it.

This activity highlights the difference between weight and volume. In solid waste, both weight and volume are a concern. When we express concern about the landfill filling up, we are discussing volume. When we pay for waste disposal, we pay for it by weight, by the ton. The trick to making this activity successful is to find a scale that is accurate to the quarter pound. While the average bathroom scale will do, the more accurately your students can weigh their materials, the more effectively they can use their math and science skills.

Materials
- ❑ Handouts
  - *Municipal Solid Waste in U.S. Landfills by Weight and Volume*
  - *Weight and Volume of Our Garbage*
- ❑ Laboratory or mail scales that read up to 10 pounds, with at least quarter-pound accuracy. If you cannot find one, use a bathroom scale.
- ❑ Calculators
- ❑ Yardstick or measuring tape
- ❑ Newspaper to spread on table or floor
- ❑ Disposable gloves (optional)
- ❑ Four pounds of "clean" (not rotten or smelly) garbage. You can collect garbage items from your own home or ask a few students to bring in one day's worth of "clean" garbage for this activity. Tell them to keep all their garbage for one day including things they would ordinarily recycle. Ask them to rinse food containers and split food and yard waste in separate bags.

Procedure
1. Separate the trash into garbage bags for as many teams of three to five students as necessary. Try to follow the ratios shown on the *Municipal Solid Waste In U.S. Landfills by Weight and Volume* handout.

2. Make an overhead of the *Municipal Solid Waste in U.S. Landfills by Weight and Volume and the Weight and Volume of Our Garbage* handouts. Ask your students to find differences between the two pie charts. They should see that weight and volume of paper, glass, plastic and yard waste differ significantly. Use the pie charts to start a discussion about the differences between weight and volume.

3. Break the class into groups of three to five students and give each group a bag of garbage. Have one recorder for each group. Set the scale in a convenient location in the classroom. Distribute calculators.

4. Have each group spread newspaper on a desk or on the floor and follow the directions on the handouts.

5. Students then empty the contents onto the newspaper and categorize the items in the garbage. They will identify each item and place it into the proper category. The recorder will record the number of items in each category.

6. Following the instructions on the handout, have students total the number of items in each category. By counting the number of items in each category and using calculators to divide that number by all the items in the garbage can, they can determine the relative percentage for each category. Assist your students with figuring out percentages.

7. When they have finished sorting the items by category, students then weigh each category of items and record the weights. Be sure all the students practice using the scale and getting the most accurate reading possible for each weight. To determine the percentage by weight, divide the weight of one category by the total garbage weight.

For example, if glass weighs 2 pounds and the total garbage weight is 4 pounds, then glass composes .5 of the total weight. Multiplying this number by 100 gives the percentage of glass in the total weight (50 percent).

8. When finished, have students make a bar chart illustrating the percentage of items in each category they found. Have them make a second bar chart to illustrate the percentage weights of the items. Are the percentages of weight and volume the same? Use the results to start a discussion about the difference between weight and volume.

9. Have the students show their bar charts to each other. Were all the bags of garbage the same? How do the relative percentages compare to each other? Different lifestyles can make for different waste compositions. What can you guess about the people who produced the garbage?

Discussion Questions

- Discuss the results. Ask your students to discuss how they compare to the national average illustrated on the overhead. What items took up the most space, or volume? What items were most numerous? Which were the heaviest?

- All garbage is compacted before going into the landfill. After estimating the garbage volume, predict how much you think compaction would change the volume. Will it affect the weight? Compact the garbage by stomping on it and take the

measurements for weight and volume again. The weight should remain the same but the volume will change.

- Discuss how recycling must change the composition of garbage going to the landfill dramatically. How would waste composition change if everyone recycled?

Modifications/Extensions

- Repeat the study after removing all the items that are normally recycled in your community recycling program. Make new bar graphs, and discuss the changes in waste composition. After recycling, what is the greatest component of solid waste? By how much did your class reduce the total volume and weight of the waste from recycling?

- For more advanced students, teach them how to make pie charts, like those on the handout. How do their pie charts compare to the national averages?

- To simplify this activity, you can leave out the comparison of weight and volume and have students simply count the items and determine their percentages by quantity.

Municipal Solid Waste in U.S. Landfills by Weight and Volume

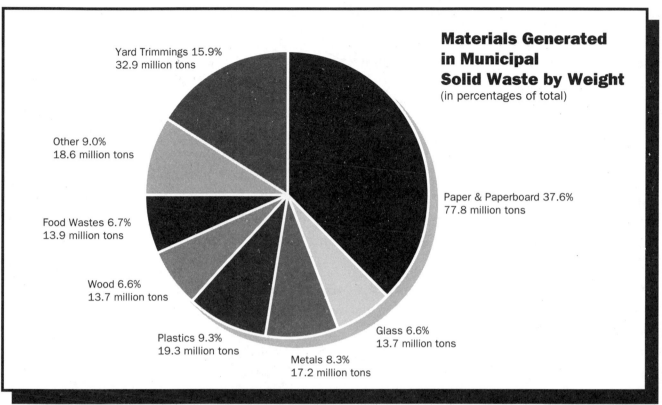

Materials Generated in Municipal Solid Waste by Weight
(in percentages of total)

Yard Trimmings 15.9%
32.9 million tons

Other 9.0%
18.6 million tons

Food Wastes 6.7%
13.9 million tons

Wood 6.6%
13.7 million tons

Plastics 9.3%
19.3 million tons

Metals 8.3%
17.2 million tons

Glass 6.6%
13.7 million tons

Paper & Paperboard 37.6%
77.8 million tons

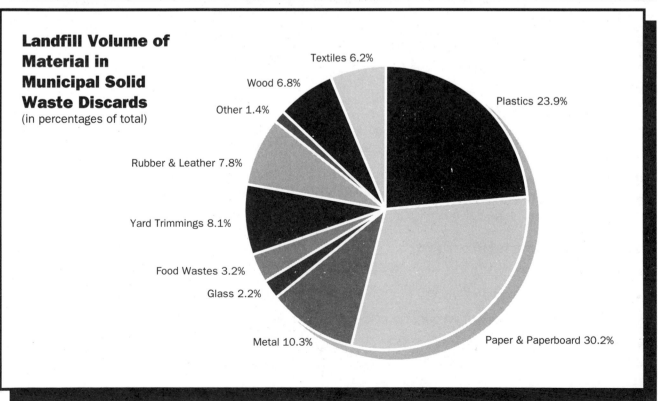

Landfill Volume of Material in Municipal Solid Waste Discards
(in percentages of total)

Textiles 6.2%

Wood 6.8%

Other 1.4%

Rubber & Leather 7.8%

Yard Trimmings 8.1%

Food Wastes 3.2%

Glass 2.2%

Metal 10.3%

Plastics 23.9%

Paper & Paperboard 30.2%

U.S. Environmental Protection Agency, 1994

Weight and Volume of Our Garbage

Name _____

1. Write down the weight of the bag:
_____ lbs. _____ oz.

2. Estimate the volume of the bag.
Measure the height of the bag, the width of the bag in both directions and multiplying the height times the width (H x W x W = Volume).
Write the estimate of volume here:

_____

3. Categorize and count.
Remove all the items and place them in categories. Write the number of each item below:
Paper _____
Metal _____
Glass _____
Plastic _____
Food/yard wastes _____
Other _____

4. Weigh-In
Weigh each category.
Paper _____ lbs _____oz
Metal _____ lbs _____oz
Glass _____ lbs _____oz
Plastic _____ lbs _____oz
Food/yard wastes _____ lbs _____oz
Other _____ lbs _____oz

5. Sum-Up
Add up the weights of the categories:
_____ lbs _____oz

6. Does it match the total weight
(from Step 1)? _____

7. Volume
Estimate the volume of each category by placing the items as close together as possible and multiplying the width by height of the garbage.

Paper _____ square inches
Metal _____ sq. in.
Glass _____ sq. in.
Plastic _____ sq. in.
Food/yard wastes _____ sq. in.
Other _____ sq. in.
Percent Paper _____
Percent Plastic _____
Percent Metals _____
Percent Food waste _____
Percent Glass _____
Percent Other _____

8. Percentage of Volume
To estimate the percent volume, divide the volume for each category by the total volume that you figured out in Step 2.
Percent Paper _____
Percent Plastic _____
Percent Metals _____
Percent Food waste _____
Percent Glass _____
Percent Other _____
Sum up. Add up the percentages here

Check to be sure that the percentages add up to 100%.

9. Follow Up
a. Which category of items weighed the most?

b. Which category of items took up the most volume? _____

c. How do your figures compare to the national averages? _____

_____

_____

Animal Tracks Activity Guide

2. Recycling Relay

Subjects:
Language Arts, Physical Education

Process Skills:
Identifying, classifying, decision-making, team work

Grades:
2–4

Cognitive Task Level:
Easy

Time for Activity:
15 to 20 minutes

Key Vocabulary:
Aluminum, glass, steel, plastic, garbage, paper, recycle

Intended Learning Outcomes:
Completing this activity will allow students to:
- Gain skill at determining what is recyclable in their recycling program
- Develop motor skills and enjoy a fun outdoor activity.

Background

This relay race challenges students to learn which items are recyclable and which are garbage. It's designed for curbside recycling programs, but can be modified to fit any area and any recycling program. This relay race should be conducted outside on the grass. Be sure to prepare your students in advance by reviewing with them the items that are recyclable in your area.

Materials

- ❑ Whistle (optional)
- ❑ Three curbside recycling bins
- ❑ Three classroom garbage cans or similar containers
- ❑ Four empty boxes
- ❑ Relay materials:
  - ❑ Four examples of all materials collected in the local curbside recycling program, as well as some things that are not. Recyclable items include PET soda bottles, aluminum cans, glass bottles, newspapers, steel cans and HDPE plastic milk jugs. Items that may not be recyclable include paper milk or juice containers, some magazines, juice boxes and empty motor oil containers.

Procedure

1. Place one of each of the items listed above into each of the four boxes. Keep one of the four boxes.

2. Have the class go outside to a grassy area or field. Select three referees. Select three team leaders and have them select their teams.

3. From where the teams will start, place the recycling bins and trash cans at the "End" (about 100 feet away). Place one set of recycling bins and one trash can for each team. Have the referees stay at the end. Be sure the referees know the goals of the game, and understand which items are to be placed in the garbage can and which are to be placed in the recycling bin.

4. Place the three large boxes with all the items listed above about 30 feet away from the "Start."

5. The teacher stands over the fourth box. He/she reaches in, holds up one item and says "go." That signals that the first team member must run to the team's box, reach in and grab the item the teacher is holding and run to the end. The student must place the item in the correct container (either the recycling bin or the trash can). Then, the team member runs as fast as possible back to start and slaps the hand of the next person. By then, the teacher holds up the next item and the next person grabs that item, runs to the end, disposes of it properly and runs back, and so on. Incorrectly placed items are returned to the box and must be disposed of again, thus slowing down the entire team. The winning team is the one that properly disposes of all its items first.

6. The referee makes sure the item is properly disposed of in the trash or in the correct recycling bin. For each item correctly disposed of, the team gets one point. Continue until all the items have been properly placed in the correct containers.

Extensions/Modifications

- To further complicate the game, add other items that are more confusing. Call your local recycling center and find out if there is a guide to curbside recycling for your area.

3. Start With Your Own Lunch

Subjects:
Environmental Science, Math, Language Arts

Process Skills:
Observing, identifying, recording, making decisions, effecting personal change

Grades:
3–6

Cognitive Task Level:
Average

Time for Activity:
15 minutes after several lunch periods

Key Vocabulary:
Compost, landfill, packaging, recycle, reduce, replace, reuse, source reduction

Intended Learning Outcomes:
Completing this activity will allow students to:

- Take a survey of the items in their lunch boxes and observe what they're packaged in
- Consider less wasteful packaging alternatives
- Create bar graphs to see the difference they can make in the amount of waste they produce by making small simple changes.

Background

There is no "away." The garbage we throw away actually goes to a sanitary landfill. Because we throw away so much garbage, our landfills are filling up at an alarming rate. Unnecessary waste comes from over-packaging, uneaten food, not reusing durable products like bags and containers and from not recycling containers that can be recycled. A look at the typical student lunch shows that everyone contributes to the garbage crisis.

In the past, people produced much less garbage. Thermoses carried drinks, bottles and cans were recycled, lunch boxes were reused and food waste was composted. We can still use these waste-reduction techniques today. The goal of this lesson is to practice source reduction in a small way. Even small changes can result in big changes in attitudes and awareness.

Materials

❑ Handout
- *My Lunch Tally Sheet*

Procedure

1. Prepare an example of a lunch box filled with disposable items that produce unnecessary waste. Prepare a second one with examples of recyclable/reusable alternatives for the wasteful items. Use the "What Can I Replace It With?" section on the handout to get some ideas.

2. Tell your students to bring their lunch waste to class after lunch, including all leftover food, plastic bags, paper bags, dishes, beverage containers and napkins.

3. Hand out the *My Lunch Tally Sheet* for Day 1. Under "Items from my lunch" column, have them list every item that they would have thrown away, including uneaten food, napkins, plastic bags, beverage containers, plastic plates or boxes, apple cores, orange peels, etc. In order to have an effective experiment, every single item must be listed!

4. For each item listed, enter the appropriate check or response in the following six columns. For example, a plastic container could be reused, or perhaps is already being reused. A juice box is garbage and must go "away" to the landfill. Next time it could be replaced with something reusable, like a thermos, or recyclable, like an aluminum can or glass bottle.

5. Discuss with the students how they can create a garbage-free lunch. Use your sample lunch box to show them how you replaced disposable items with reusable and recyclable ones. Make an overhead transparency of the "What Can I Replace It With?" section of the handout and use this to help your students come up with their own ideas.

6. Discuss composting with your students. All food waste can be composted, except meats, cheese and very oily items, like a mayonnaise-slathered piece of bread. Your class may want to try starting a bucket of compost in the classroom to compost such food waste as fruits, vegetables and grains. See the "Owl Unit — Composting" for more ideas. Untouched food may be donated to a food bank.

7. Continue the experiment for at least three days. Students should replace disposable items with reusables, and reuse these items each day, indicating this on their tally sheets.

8. At the end of three days, have students tally up the totals in each column for each day. Have them draw a graph that shows these totals. The number of items thrown "away" should decrease and the number of items reused or recycled will increase over the period. The student will see that he or she made a big difference in the amount of garbage he or she produces.

9. Repeat this activity periodically throughout the school year.

Extensions/Modifications

- Make a large poster illustrating the results of this activity. Have it displayed in a prominent place in the school, encouraging other classes to reduce their lunch-time garbage. Or make a school-wide policy to reward students who have garbage-free lunches. Be sure the reward does not produce more garbage! A cloth lunch bag or extra recess time would be a suitable reward.

My Lunch Tally Sheet

Name _____

Day	Lunch item	What material is it made from?	Disposable	Reusable	Recyclable	Is it reused from previous day?	Less wasteful alternative
1	**Sample** juice bottle	plastic		✓		No	Thermos or glass bottle

What can I replace it with?

Disposable Item	Replace with
Paper bag	Reusable bag or lunch box
Paper napkin	Cloth napkin
Disposable drink container	Thermos, recyclable glass or aluminum, reusable plastic
Plastic baggie	Rinse and reuse
Disposable box or plate	Reusable container, like reusable margarine tub or yogurt container
Individual packages (chips, raisins, cupcakes)	Buy in bulk. Less packaging and cheaper, too! Reuse the bag.
Uneaten food	Save for next day or donate to food bank
Food waste: Apple cores, banana peel, crackers, etc.	Compost

4. On the Recycling Road

Subjects:
Social Studies, Language Arts, Economics, Math

Process Skills:
Following directions, observing, cooperative learning

Grades:
3–8

Time for Activity:
20 minutes

Cognitive Task Level:
Average

Key Vocabulary:
Materials recovery facility, manufacturing plant

Intended Learning Outcomes:
Completing this activity will allow students to:
- Learn about the steps involved in the process of recycling
- Interact cooperatively with other students
- Play an enjoyable educational game.

Background
The recycling process is a difficult one to explain unless all the steps are clearly understood. This game takes students through the steps of recycling, while allowing them to experience the trials and tribulations of the recycling process in a fun setting.

Materials
- ❑ Handouts
    - *On The Recycling Road* board game (one copy for each group of four students)
- ❑ Players' pieces
- ❑ One die for each group of four

Procedure
1. Make copies of the game and players' pieces. Cut out the players' pieces and give one of each type to each group. Divide your class into groups of four students, and distribute the game and players. Let the students pick which player they choose to be.

2. Review the rules:
- Only a roll of 1, 2 or 3 can be used. A student who rolls a number greater than 3 must wait until the next turn.
- Players must go through the recycling process three times before they are finished. The first student who goes through the recycling process three times is the winner.

3. Follow up the game with a discussion about what the students learned. Ask them what part they enjoyed most. Did this activity help them understand how the recycling process works?

(*On The Recycling Road* is adapted with permission from the Sacramento County Recycling Program Social Studies Curriculum for Middle Grades.)

Resources for Recycling Plastics and Glass
- *Sand Lab Kit* (Math Science Nucleus, 3710 Yale Way, Fremont, CA 94538; 415-490-MATH).
- *Complete Glass Kit* (Glass Packaging Institute. 1801 K St., NW Washington, DC 20006; 202-887-4850).
- *Polymer Chemistry, Revised Edition. A Teaching Package for Pre-College Teachers.* (National Science Teachers Association, 1742 Connecticut Avenue, NW Washington, DC 20009).

On The Recycling Road

Players

Teacher: Photocopy this page and have your students cut out their own players.
Or, laminate a set on colored paper to use over again.

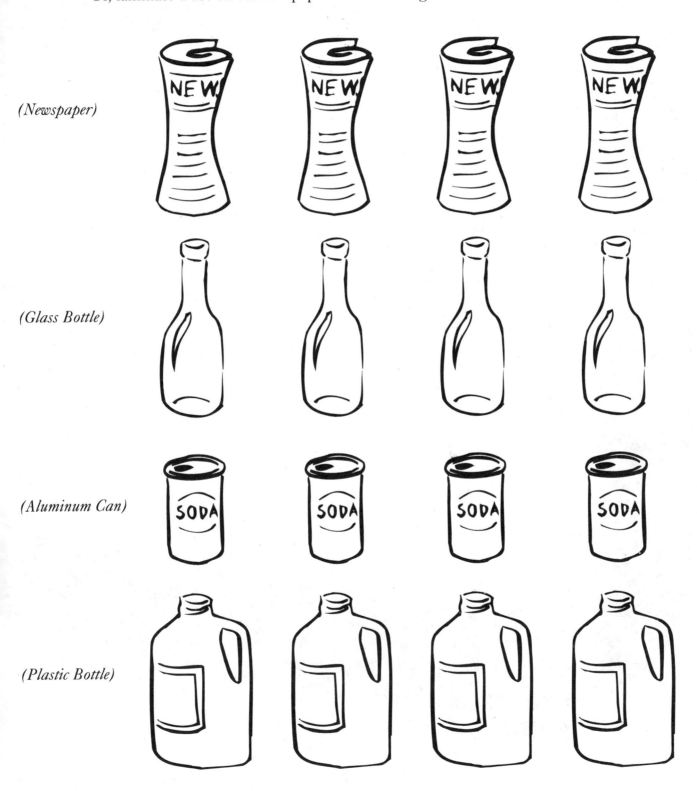

(Newspaper)

(Glass Bottle)

(Aluminum Can)

(Plastic Bottle)

Materials Processing Facility

Wait 1 turn.

Materials Processing Facility

Move forward 2 spaces.

You have been loaded for shipping

UH, OH! You fell off the truck and are now litter!

RETURN TO START!

You made it in curbside recycling.

HOORAY! Roll again.

Placed in trash and taken to landfill...

START OVER!

Recycling bin not placed correctly on curb.

Lose 1 turn!

On the Red

Now you're home!

Home

Recycling Plant

ycling Road

Grocery Store

CONGRATS! You have reached the Recycling Plant. GO AGAIN.

Waiting for a buyer. Wait 1 turn.

Low Market Value.

Return to Recycling Plant

Broken in Shipping.

Move ahead 1 space!

Delivered by truck to Grocery Store.

In Storage. Waiting fo to be placed on shelf

Wait 1 turn.

ROLL AGAIN.

TADA! You are now on the shelf!

Move ahead 1 space.

Rules:

Only 1, 2, or 3 on the die.

You must go through the game 3 times.

The first person who goes through the game 3 times, WINS!!

Composting

The Challenge

We throw away lots of things that could actually help the earth if they didn't end up in a landfill. Most of the food we throw away, branches and trimmings from trees and other yard waste gets mixed up with all our other garbage. It fills about a quarter of all the landfill space.

This is the kind of garbage we can mix together and let decompose, or break down. If it's done right, it doesn't smell. And in a short time, the eggshells, carrot peelings and leaves actually break down to become a great mixture to add to the soil in your flower bed or garden.

The funny thing is that not too many Americans compost, but we do spend millions of dollars each year to buy topsoil and fertilizers to make our flower beds prettier and our gardens more productive.

Think of it. We're paying money to haul away the kind of materials that make the nutrients we pay to spread in our yards. If we all start composting, we'll save twice. Once, in the space we save in our landfills. And second, in the money we don't spend to either haul away "good" garbage or buy chemicals.

Did You Know?

- Americans throw out 13 million tons of food waste each year. That's a lot of chicken bones, apple cores and lettuce leaves!
- Organic matter, which is yard and food waste does not decompose in a landfill. Nothing breaks down in landfills because there is not enough moisture and oxygen to feed the process of decomposition.
- Allowing grass clippings to remain on the lawn reduces water evaporation (which dries out the grass) and reduces erosion of topsoil. Erosion occurs as soil moves from where it should be. Erosion makes a river look like chocolate milk after a rainstorm because soil has washed off the land and into the water.
- Burning yard waste isn't a very environmentally healthy option. Every ton of leaves we burn releases 120 pounds of carbon monoxide and other particles that are unhealthy to breathe.

The Composting chapter of the *Animal Tracks Activity Guide* corresponds to the Owl chapter of the *Animal Tracks* children's book.

1. Wild Animals in Soil

Subjects:
Science, Environmental Science, Language Arts, Art

Process Skills:
Collecting data, following directions, writing observations, finding similarities and differences between organisms, categorizing organisms, drawing organisms

Grades:
3–6

Cognitive Task Level:
Average

Time for Activity:
One to two 50-minute class periods

Key Vocabulary:
Decomposer, dichotomous key, food web, invertebrate, litter

Intended Learning Outcomes:
Completing this activity will allow students to:

- Collect leaf litter and examine the animals that live on the forest floor
- Receive an introduction to methods of classification used by scientists (dichotomous key)
- Observe the abundance and diversity of organisms to be found in a small sample of earth.

Background
When we think of animals and nature, we usually think of the large, beautiful mammals we see most often on nature shows or the smaller mammals that occur in our own neighborhoods, like raccoons, opossums, cats, dogs and squirrels. These warm-blooded vertebrates are most similar to ourselves.

In fact, 97 percent of all the animals on earth are invertebrates, or animals without backbones. Many of these animals are also decomposers, which consume organic matter and convert it into a form that provides nutrients for plants. Without decomposers, all life on earth would soon end because we would drown in an ocean of organic waste. Imagine if every leaf that fell from a tree was still on the ground! This activity also provides an introduction to a classic method of classification, the dichotomous (two-option) key and an opportunity to use field guides to identify the insects found.

Materials
- ❑ Large jar
- ❑ Small bucket
- ❑ Trowel
- ❑ Leaf litter
- ❑ Large funnel
- ❑ 3/4" Wire mesh cut into a circle to fit into the funnel, about 2 inches from the top of the funnel
- ❑ Gooseneck lamp
- ❑ *Field Guide to Insects*
- ❑ Handout:
  - *Wild Animals in Soil*

Procedure
1. If possible, conduct a nature walk in a park or wild area near the school. If no place is available for a nature walk, collect some leaf litter elsewhere and bring it to school. Collect the leaf litter no more than 24 hours in advance and keep it cool and dark until you use it in the classroom. Collect several trowels full of leaf litter. Try to get damp leaves or soil.

2. In the classroom, set the funnel in the glass jar and place the screen inside the funnel so that it's about two inches below the lip of the funnel. Dump the leaf litter onto the screen. Place the lamp and turn it on to shine over the litter. After about an hour, the heat from the lamp will drive animals in the soil down through the leaves. They will fall through the mesh and down the funnel into the jar.

3. Using a *Field Guide to Insects* and the Wild Animals in Soil handout, have the students identify as many animals as they can. Use physical characteristics, like the number of legs and body segments or the presence or absence of antennae to help categorize the animals. Count and chart the number of each kind.

Extensions/Modifications
- To simplify this activity, collect the animals and look at them, comparing their similarities and differences without the data sheet.
- To expand this lesson for more advanced students, use a comprehensive dichotomous key, available in some insect guides, for students to key invertebrates to the correct genus or species.

Wild Animals in Soil

Name _____

Follow the clues provided to help you find out what type of animal you're seeing.
Then, look in the *Field Guide to Insects* for more specific information about your wild animal.

A Branching Key

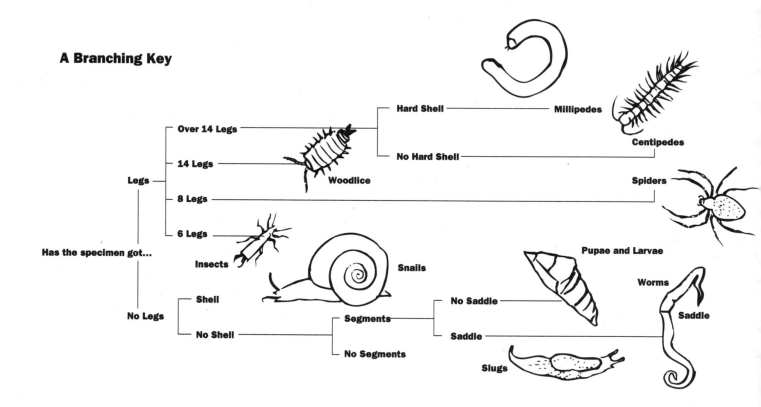

2. Cooking Compost

Subjects:

Science, Environmental Science, Language Arts, Art, Health

Process Skills:

Making comparisons over time, synthesizing observations, writing instructions, illustrating

Grades:

3–6

Cognitive Task Level:

Simple

Time for Activity:

10 to 15 minutes every other day for two weeks

Key Vocabulary:

Actinomycetes, bacteria, compost, decompose, fungi, humus, microorganisms, organic

Intended Learning Outcomes:

Completing this activity will allow students to:

- Learn how to make compost
- Observe the process of decomposition and observe the effects of invisible microorganisms in organic matter
- Describe the composting process by writing and illustrating creative recipe cards.

Background

Soil is an important natural resource. It contains the minerals and nutrients plants need to grow. Soil is composed of rocks, minerals and humus, the byproduct of decomposed organic matter. In the soil are tiny, microscopic animals that eat dead organic matter and convert it into a form easily absorbed by plants. These microorganisms are the most numerous creatures in the world. One handful of soil can contain five billion creatures!

Composting is the process people use to convert organic matter to humus. It can happen anywhere there is sufficient organic matter, moisture and air to nurture the microscopic bacteria, fungi and actinomycetes that break down organic matter. As master composters everywhere say, "Compost Happens!"

Materials

- [ ] One reusable cup per student
- [ ] Scissors
- [ ] Rubber bands for each student
- [ ] Nylon window screen material (available at hardware stores)
- [ ] Soil, compost or dirt
- [ ] Plant wastes: fruit or vegetable pieces and skins, grasses, weeds or leaves
- [ ] Plant sprayer
- [ ] 3-inch x 5-inch notecards or recipe cards
- [ ] Handout:
  - *Decomposers and Compost*

Procedure

1. Start this activity with a discussion of the major players involved in making compost. The *Decomposers and Compost* handout includes an introduction to the common decomposers always present in soil. While some bacteria and fungi are considered harmful to humans, the bacteria, molds, fungi and actinomycetes (a microorganism that decomposes organic matter) found in soil are what cause the decomposition process. Without them, our world would be so full of dead leaves, animals, food wastes and yard debris that all other life would soon be buried!

2. Distribute cups, scissors and the handouts to the students. Cut the nylon screen into pieces large enough to cover the top of the cup and be secured by the rubber band. Distribute one piece of screen and one rubber band to each student.

3. Have each student place about two tablespoons of soil in their cup.

4. Using the scissors, have students cut the plant wastes into small pieces. The smaller the pieces, the faster the results. Pack the plant wastes loosely in the cup. Do not use meats, oils or animal byproducts in compost. They produce an unpleasant odor when they decompose.

5. Spray enough water into the cup to moisten the contents and mix thoroughly. Cover with the nylon screen and secure with the rubber band.

6. Every day or two, stir contents of cup and spray with water to keep soil moist, but not wet. If the soil is too wet or too dry, the bacteria will not function as efficiently. Have your students record their observations on the *Decomposers and Compost* data sheet.

7. Within two to three weeks, the organic matter will decompose into rich, dark brown humus. As your students observe the contents of the cups transform from plant matter to nutritious humus, ask them what they think happened. Although the decomposers are not visible to the naked eye, the evidence of their activity is apparent. What can they deduce from the composting process? Do they realize that microorganisms are eating the organic matter, digesting it and excreting it as humus? Ask them what they think the decomposers look like. If you have pictures of bacteria, fungi and molds, display them.

8. Have your students write and illustrate a composting recipe card. Instruct them on the proper recipe card format, and have them use their imaginations to write the instructions for cooking compost. Have them illustrate the cards with a picture of what they imagine a decomposer looks like, or have them illustrate a step from the instructions on their recipe cards.

Extensions/Modifications

- Your class can conduct indoor composting on a larger scale using a bucket. Follow the same instructions as for the activity above. Add a thermometer to check the temperature. Compost in the bucket should show a higher temperature in the center of the bucket. This is another indicator that organisms are working, eating and generating heat.

- Conduct a series of experiments with your compost. Use different types of soil, including sawdust, sterilized potting soil (in which the microorganisms have been killed), previously composted soil, etc. Also try keeping the compost very dry, very wet and at a moderate moisture level. See which compost combinations work most effectively and have your students write up their results.

Teacher's Version

Answer to *Macroorganism Question* (on Decomposers and Compost)

Macroorganisms are earthworm, sow bug, beetle and centipede.
(The bacteria, molds and fungi, and actinomycetes are microorganisms.)

Decomposers and Compost

Name _____

Cookin' Compost

Ingredients: _____
_____
_____
_____
_____

Directions: _____
_____
_____
_____
_____
_____

DAY 1: Describe what you did. What types of plant materials did you put in the cup? _____

_____

One week later: Describe what you see, feel and smell. _____

_____

Two weeks later: Describe what you see, feel and smell. _____

_____

What caused this change to happen? _____

_____

Write down any other observations you made from this experiment. _____

_____

Decomposers and Compost *(Continued)*

Common Decomposers

Decomposers are animals that break down organic matter by eating it, digesting it and excreting it in a form that can be used by plants. They are some of the most important animals on earth. Without them, we would all soon be buried in leaves and grass! The organisms shown here do all the work in the compost pile, breaking down the dead material to form rich humus.

Most decomposers are so small that they are called microorganisms. They can only be seen under a microscope. Other organisms are large enough to be seen. These are called macroorganisms. Below, write the names of the macroorganisms that you can see in the picture.

_____   _____

_____   _____

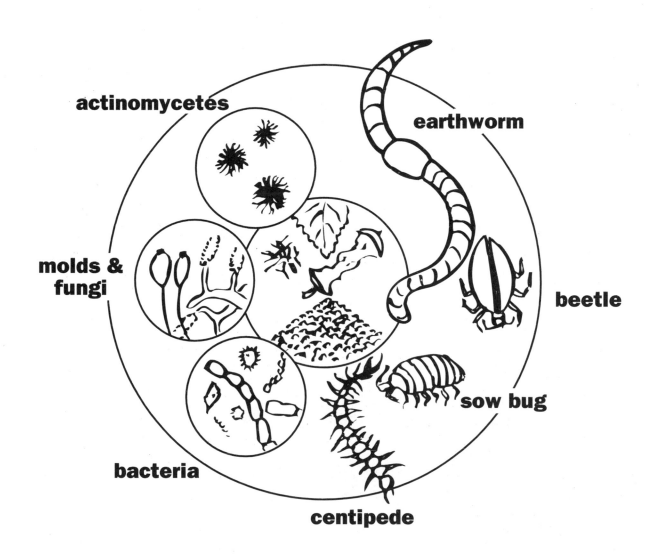

3. Vermicomposting

Subjects:
Science, Social Studies, Environmental Science, Economics

Process Skills:
Making comparisons over time, synthesizing observations, writing instructions, illustrating

Grades:
3–6

Cognitive Task Level:
Simple

Time for Activity:
10 to 15 minutes every other day for two weeks

Key Vocabulary:
Compost, decompose, macroorganisms, vermicomposting

Intended Learning Outcomes:
Completing this activity will allow students to:
- Participate in the process by which macroorganisms convert large quantities of food and yard waste into rich humus
- Observe the life cycle of the worm, Eisenia fetida
- Become caretakers and stewards of live animals.

Background

Food and yard waste compose 25 percent of the solid waste in landfills. This figure can rise to a high of 40 percent in some areas and during certain seasons. It's a well-established fact that biodegradation does not occur in landfills, as there are not sufficient air and moisture to encourage the proliferation of the aerobic microorganisms that are the major decomposers in nature.

Modern sanitary landfills are presently the most efficient and safest way to dispose of non-recyclable, non-biodegradable waste items, but organic material can be disposed of much more effectively by composting. Vermicomposting is one method of converting food and yard waste into rich, nutritious compost that can be reused on gardens and landscaping. This keeps organic waste out of the landfill, too.

Vermicomposting is commonly called worm composting. Using a specific species of worm, *Eisenia fetida*, food waste is converted into rich, earthy humus. Worm composting is a fairly simple activity that can be conducted in the classroom. Students are able to observe the life cycle of the worm as well as the transformation worms perform on food waste.

Materials
- ❑ 1/2 to 1 pound of worms (see "Sources for worms" at end of "Procedure" section)
- ❑ Large polystyrene ice chest or worm composting bin
- ❑ Newspaper
- ❑ Spray bottles
- ❑ Food waste (include a variety, such as fruit peels, vegetable skins, grains, egg shells and tea bags, but avoid citrus rinds, meats, oils and milk products)
- ❑ Handout
  - *Vermicomposting Worksheet*

Procedure

1. Not all worms are the best worms for composting food waste. *Eisenia fetida*, also commonly known as the red worm, red wiggler, manure worm and English red worm, is the best worm for this purpose. The easiest way to acquire them is through mail-order catalogs and businesses. Costs range from $15 to $30 per pound of worms, and they arrive with care instructions.

2. Your worms need a home in the classroom. Many of the mail-order businesses sell worm composting bins that are specially designed for the worms. If you don't get one of these, use a large polystyrene cooler or glass aquarium.

3. Line the bottom of the worm bin with shredded newspaper or other discarded waste paper. Place at least four inches on the bottom of the bin. Spray the paper thoroughly with water so it's saturated.

4. Before placing your worms in the bin, pour them out onto a newspaper so your class can get a good look at them. The worms are reddish-brown, about two inches long and will probably be quite active. They will arrive in some of their own compost. Look for new worms which look just like adults but are smaller. You may also see thin white worms. These worms live with the redworms and also decompose organic matter. Worm egg cases are about the size of the head of a pin. Have your class write their observations on the *Vermicomposting Worksheets*.

5. When all observations have been made, have your students scoop up the worms and compost and place them gently onto the newspaper bedding. Add your food waste now. Cover the worms with more damp shredded paper. Place a cover loosely over the top of the bin. As long as the worms have enough food to eat, air to breathe and aren't drowning in standing water, they should remain healthy in the bin.

6. Check the worms regularly, at least every other day. Keep the newspaper moist, but not wet. After one week, have your students complete their worksheets by writing down their observations.

7. After a few weeks, you may notice that the newspaper bedding is disappearing or that the bin is getting full of compost. To harvest your compost and provide new bedding to replace what the worms have consumed, pour the worms onto some newspaper. Take some time to compare the worm population with the previous observations. If the worms are happy and healthy, you will see many worm egg cases and more worms than you started with. Fewer worms suggests that the population isn't healthy or there isn't enough food for everyone.

8. You will notice that the worms avoid the light and burrow into the compost. To harvest the compost, shine a bright light on the worms to force them to burrow even faster. After a few minutes, nearly all the worms will be at the bottom of the pile. Have your students carefully scoop the finished compost off the top. Continue this until you have harvested as much compost as possible without collecting too many worms.

9. Start your compost bin again by repeating the instructions above. Apply the finished compost to plants in the classroom or school yard.

Worm Sources:

- Flowerfield Enterprises, 10332 Shaver Road, Kalamazoo, MI 49002; 616-327-0108. Offers a worm composting starter kit, or you can just order worms.
- Gardener's Supply Co., 128 Intervale Road, Burlington, VT 05401; 800-955-3370.
- Smith & Hawken, Two Arbor Lane, Box 6900, Florence, KY 41022-6900; 800-776-3336.
- Seventh Generation, Colchester, VT 05446-1672; 800-456-1177.
- Worm's Way, 3151 South Highway 446, Bloomington, ID 47401; 800-274-9676.

Extensions/Modifications

- Weigh the food waste you give the worms and observe how long it takes them to consume it.

Vermicomposting Worksheet

Name _____

1. Write down a description of what you see. _____
_____
_____
_____

Draw a picture of the worms.

2. What do the worms need to survive? Describe the container your class has prepared
for the worms. _____
_____
_____

3. What do you feed your worms? Write down all the things your class placed in the worm bin.

_____   _____
_____   _____
_____   _____
_____   _____
_____   _____

4. After one week, look at your worms. Describe what foods have disappeared. Describe any
changes you see in the bin. What's been added? Is it getting dry? Does it need water? Are the
worms getting enough air? _____

_____
_____
_____
_____

4. Outdoor Composting

Subjects:
Environmental Science, Social Studies, Gardening

Process Skills:
Recording observations, gardening, comparing, using a thermometer

Grades:
3–6

Cognitive Task Level:
Simple to average

Time for Activity:
15 minutes once per week

Key Vocabulary:
Compost, decomposition, humus, microorganisms, organic

Intended Learning Outcomes:
Completing this activity will allow students to:
- Learn how to build a compost container
- Maintain a compost pile and observe changes over time
- Record and document the changes they observe in a compost diary.

Background

Natural microorganisms and decomposers occur anywhere there is organic matter. Any dirt or open grassy area is full of them. An outdoor compost container open at the bottom allows these decomposers to travel up into the organic yard waste placed in the compost container. Decomposers are "aerobic." They need oxygen to breathe as well as moisture. An outdoor compost container made of inexpensive wire mesh creates the right conditions for the aerobic breakdown of organic matter.

All you need to do to help your class observe decomposition is to provide the dirt area and wire. Your students can make the compost containers, set them up in the soil, collect the organic debris and add water. Within two weeks, they will observe their efforts form rich humus, the soil additive which provides nutrients to growing plants. By combining this activity with a gardening activity, your students will gain an understanding of the cycles of nature, including decomposition and growth.

Materials

- [ ] To make compost container:
  - [ ] 2 yards of 1-inch gauge wire mesh per group
  - [ ] Pliers
- [ ] Yard waste from the school grounds
- [ ] Garden tools for turning compost (trowels, pitchforks, etc.)
- [ ] Small diary or notebook
- [ ] Outdoor thermometer or kitchen thermometer
- [ ] Handout:
  - *Guide to Outdoor Composting*

Procedure

1. Have your students work in pairs or threes to make their compost containers. To make a simple outdoor compost container, use 2 yards of 1-inch gauge wire mesh (chicken wire). Roll the mesh into a circle. Using a pliers, fold the loose ends of the wire on one edge over the edge of the other to secure the circle.

2. Find a suitable outdoor spot on the school grounds to place the compost containers so they're in contact with the soil.

3. Distribute the Guide to Outdoor Composting. Have your class collect yard waste from the custodian or school landscaper. If your school doesn't have anyone who tends the landscaping, offer to have your class start weeding, pruning, sweeping leaves and tending the plants and trees. Collect the leftover yard clippings for the compost containers. Cut larger clippings to smaller size. The smaller the pieces, the more quickly they will decompose.

4. Have your students start piling the yard waste in their compost containers. About once a week, collect more yard waste and add it to the pile. Turn and mix the yard materials well and sprinkle lightly with water. After about two weeks, you should begin to notice changes in the compost piles. The colorful plant materials will fade, turning brown. The pile will become compact as microorganisms begin to break down the material and reduce air pockets.

5. Have your students keep a diary of the process. Each time they work on their compost containers or project, have them write a paragraph of notes describing what they did and what they learned or observed.

6. After three weeks, you should notice significant changes in the compost piles. If there is little change and the yard materials seem to be unchanged, see the Guide to Outdoor Composting. Have your students place the thermometer into their compost piles to see if the activity of the microorganisms feeding on the organic waste has increased the temperature of the pile.

7. Compost piles can be worked for the entire year, spending about 15 minutes, once per week. By combining this activity with other garden activities, you can develop a comprehensive environmental science component as part of the regular curriculum.

Extensions/Modifications

- For a smaller-scale activity, use plastic restaurant supply buckets with the bottoms cut out for the compost containers.
- A very simple compost pile can be created by simply piling organic waste onto a specific area. Over time, nature's decomposers will find the pile and start to decompose the materials. Students can take turns turning and maintaining the pile.
- Contact the local gardening association or recycling program to find out if a speaker can come to the class and help the students get started on their compost piles.

Resources for Composting
Books for Adults

- *Home Composting*, Seattle Tilth Association (4649 Sunnyside Ave., N. Seattle, WA 98103. Cost is $2.50 plus a self-addressed envelope stamped with 50¢ postage).
- *The Chemical-Free Lawn*, by Warren Schultz, Rodale Press, Emmaus, PA.
- *Worms Eat My Garbage*, by Mary Applehof, Flower Press, Kalamazoo, MI.

Books for Students

- *Bugs*, by Nancy Winslow Parker and Joan Richards Wright. A Mulberry Paperback Book, New York. A well-illustrated book about common bugs that clearly identifies body parts and provides natural history information.
- *Squirmy Wormy Composters*. Crabtree Publishing Company, New York. A fun book about worm composting.
- *Wonderful Worms*, by Linda Glaser. The Millbrook Press, Brookfield CT. A good read-aloud book about earthworms, which includes worm facts and information.

Curriculum

- *Worms Eat Our Garbage: Classroom Activities for A Better Environment*, by Mary Frances Fenton and Barbara Loss Harris. Flower Field Enterprises, 10332 Shaver Road, Kalamazoo, MI 49002, 616-327-0108.

Video and Audio

- The Banana Slug String Band has music cassettes and a video highlighting their songs about the earth, including *Dirt Made My Lunch, Slugs at Sea, Adventures on the Air Cycle* and *Dancing with the Earth*. (PO Box 2262, Santa Cruz, CA 95063; 408-476-5776).
- *Wormania!* Flower Field Enterprises, 10332 Shaver Road, Kalamazoo, MI 49002, 616-327-0108. This 26-minute video describes the life cycle of redworms.

Guide to Outdoor Composting

Instructions:

1. Place the compost container outside on the ground or grass. This allows microorganisms from the soil to enter the pile.

2. Place discarded yard waste such as dead leaves, cut grass and pine needles into the compost bin.

3. Sprinkle with water until the pile is damp but not wet.

4. Using the pitchfork, turn the pile at least once a week to properly aerate the entire pile. Add ingredients (see below) regularly. Sprinkle with water for even moisture throughout the pile.

5. Before harvesting the compost to use as fertilizer for plants, stop adding materials at least two weeks before harvesting. Keep turning and moistening the pile until it has turned into rich, brown, earthy-smelling humus.

Animal Needs

Like most animals, the microorganisms and macroorganisms in a compost pile need air, water and a balanced diet of food nutrients, especially carbon and nitrogen. For the most efficient compost pile, place a wide variety of materials into the bin. The table below lists common compostable materials that are rich in carbon and nitrogen.

Carbon-Rich Materials
- ❑ Sawdust
- ❑ Woody plant prunings
- ❑ Pine needles
- ❑ Fallen leaves

Nitrogen-Rich Materials
- ❑ Green yard trimmings and weeds
- ❑ Grass clippings
- ❑ Coffee grounds
- ❑ Orange peels

Balanced Carbon and Nitrogen
- ❑ Most kitchen waste
- ❑ Herbivore manure (horse or cow)
- ❑ Hair clippings

Pesticides & Fertilizers

The Challenge

Chemical pesticides control pest problems. We use pesticides to remove birds, insects and bacteria we don't want. We also use pesticides to prevent diseases carried by insects and other pests. We don't just spray pesticides on farm fields. We use them in hospitals, roadways, food processing plants and yes, even our own homes. We have come to rely heavily on pesticides.

But, pesticides also kill helpful plants and animals and disrupt the natural web of life. In 1980 to 1982, California farmers sprayed Malathion to control medflies. Huge numbers of honeybees, which pollinate fruits and vegetables, were also killed.

Besides using pesticides, we also use fertilizers, which are like vitamins for plants. They help plants grow, but chemical fertilizers can upset the balance of our ecosystem by polluting our water and air.

Some things occurring in nature work like pesticides and fertilizers. Frogs and toads can act like a pesticide by eating harmful insects like cutworm which can destroy flowers and vegetables. When animal and plant matter decomposes, it acts like a fertilizer, feeding the soil and helping new plants grow.

As we have observed nature, we learned to make powerful products to mimic those processes. But, if we use natural products or smaller amounts of synthetic chemicals, we can help keep our environment healthy. So, instead of spraying the garden, invite a toad to live there!

The Pesticides & Fertilizers chapter of the *Animal Tracks Activity Guide* corresponds to the Bear chapter of the *Animal Tracks* children's book.

Did You Know?

- Pests, which are harmful insects, rodents, weeds and fungi, destroy gardens and farm crops. A single pair of aphids, which feed on apple trees and pea plants, can produce 600 billion offspring.
- In 1962, biologist Rachel Carson wrote *Silent Spring*, a book about

how pesticides also kill creatures that aren't harmful. Her book made people so concerned that we began to pass laws to control the use of some pesticides.

- In the 1970s, the pesticide DDT caused the number of peregrine falcons, bald eagles and brown pelicans to fall sharply. Farmers sprayed DDT to prevent insects from eating their crops. Rain washed the chemical into the ground and nearby lakes and rivers. Small creatures drank it, and were, in turn, eaten by pelicans and other birds. The pesticide caused the birds to lay eggs with shells so thin that they broke when the parents tried to incubate them.

- In 1972, we banned DDT from most uses in the United States. Some animal species that had been affected, like bald eagles and pelicans, have made comebacks. When farmers stopped spraying, more baby birds were born.

- For centuries, farmers have used crop rotation to keep soil productive without using chemical fertilizers. Over-use of fertilizers can actually reduce growth and productivity over time.

1. Seedlings, Fertilizers and Compost
Background
To grow, plants, like animals, require essential minerals and elements, along with sunlight and water. Many soils don't provide

Subjects:
Environmental Science, Science, Math

Process Skills:
Gardening, observing, recording, comparing, measuring

Grades:
3–6

Cognitive Task Level:
Simple to average

Time for Activity:
One 20-minute activity period a week for 10 to 12 weeks

Key Vocabulary:
Growth, fertilizer, height, compost

Intended Learning Outcomes:
Completing this activity will allow students to:
- Grow bean plants from seeds and observe the growth process
- Compare the difference in growth of plants treated with fertilizer and compost and without any additives
- Explore the complex issues associated with using fertilizers in the environment.

enough nutrients for plants to grow well. Fertilizers are like vitamins — they add nutrients to the soil. But, like vitamins, they can't replace a balanced diet. Nature's fertilizer, compost, provides a more balanced diet than synthetic fertilizer. It recycles the byproducts of dead leaves and plants into a form that can be taken up by plants again.

Fertilizers are very popular and useful in our world, but they also create environmental problems. Applying too much fertilizer means that runoff can be carried into surface waters and groundwater. Since fertilizer provides nutrients, water plants such as algae also get a boost. The excessive growth of algae can overwhelm the animals that eat algae, like fish or insects. Too much algae can block the sunlight in a stream, killing other plants below the surface. When algae dies, the decomposing plant matter actually absorbs oxygen and can suffocate fish and other plants and animals that need oxygen. In this way, fertilizers can throw the entire ecosystem out of balance. That's why compost is recommended, especially in home gardens and yards. Compost contains the right balance of nutrients and is less powerful than fertilizer. And since compost comes in the form of soil, runoff from compost is less likely to cause problems to nearby surface waters.

This activity gives students a chance to see if compost works better than synthetic fertilizers at encouraging plant growth. The results of this experiment will vary depending on soil, light conditions and the type of fertilizer and compost used.

Materials
- [ ] Rulers
- [ ] Bean seeds or similar fast-growing plant, such as coleus
- [ ] Small pots or cups (preferably reused, with a hole in the bottom)
- [ ] Purchased topsoil
- [ ] Commercial fertilizer
- [ ] Compost (either purchased or homemade)
- [ ] Sunny location
- [ ] Journals for students (optional)
- [ ] Handouts:
  - *Seedling Data Sheet*
  - *Growth Chart*

Procedure

1. On the first day, have the students break into groups of two or three. Distribute three pots and six bean seeds per group. Pass out both data sheets. Tell students to plant two bean seeds per pot. Have them label the pots 1, 2 and 3. Pot 1 will be left alone, and is called the "control." Pot 2 will have commercial fertilizer added, following the instructions on the container. Pot 3 will have compost added to the soil. Have each group label their pots so there's no confusion. Place the pots in a sunny place, and have a student monitor and water them every other day. If you choose to use a journal, have your students write down what they did in the journal.

2. Each week, preferably on the same day, have your student groups check their pots. Using the data sheets and their rulers, have your students measure their plants, fill out their data charts for the three pots and write down their observa-tions in their journals. Encourage the students to work together. For example, one student can be the recorder, while the other two mea-sure the plants. Many of the pots will have two seedlings, since two seeds were planted. Have the stu-dents divide the chart to record data about both seedlings separately; have them pull out one of the seedlings; or have them combine the measurements of the two seedlings and record the average. Whatever you decide, be sure all the students conduct the experi-ment in the same way.

3. After four weeks, have the stu-dents fill out the *Growth Chart*. You can use a different *Growth Chart* for each measurement, or just measure height of the plant. Have them use three different colors or three differ-ent types of markings to record each of the different pots of seedlings. Continue recording the results on the Growth chart every time the class measures its seedlings.

4. At the end of 10 or 12 weeks, look at the results. Based on the *Growth Charts*, could your students tell which seedlings grew the most? Was there a noticeable difference between the pots? The results will vary, so be prepared for any answer. In some cases, the pots with com-post will grow the most. In other cases, the fertilized pots will grow fastest. Explain to students that this means the fastest growing plants probably got most of the nutrients they needed. In some cases, the pots without any additives will grow the best. This indicates that the soil was already fairly nutritious before adding anything to it. Soil like this may not need additional nutrients.

5. Use this period as a chance to dis-cuss the pros and cons of synthetic fertilizers and natural compost. Would your students be willing to have their plants grow slower with compost than use synthetic fertilizer?

6. Finish the assignment by having them write a report, using the observations from their journals and their Seedling *Data and Growth* charts. Be sure they describe the purpose of the experiment, what they did and what they observed. Have them conclude with a state-ment of what they learned.

Extensions/Modifications
- This experiment can be expanded by using a variety of different types of fertilizers or natural composting materials, like mulch, bone meal, cow manure, etc. Each group can conduct a different type of experiment.
- The experiment can be speeded up by using cuttings instead of seeds.
- As a companion experiment, collect rainwater in two separate cups. Add plant food or fertilizer to one and leave the other one alone. You may observe that green algae quickly forms in the cup with fertilizer added. This is exactly what happens in surface waters where runoff from fertil-izers collect. The algae can cre-ate an imbalance in the aquatic food web.

Seedling Data Sheet

Name _____

Pot Number _____

Indicate the number of the pot — 1, 2 or 3 — for each data chart. Record your observations.

Week	Total Height	# of Leaves	Size of Leaves	# of Branches	# of Flower Buds	Color of Leaves	Other: _____ _____
1							
2							
3							
4							
5							
6							
7							
8							
9							
10							
11							
12							

Suggested observation categories:

Total height: The length of the highest tip, in inches or centimeters, of the plant above the ground.

Number of leaves: Total number of leaves on the plant.

Size of leaves: The simple measurement is small, medium or large. For more advanced experiments, measure several leaves and take the average. Measurement can be made in length, width or both.

Number of branches: The number of branching stems on the plant.

Number of flower buds: If the plant has any buds, write the total here. Many plants will not have flower buds.

Color of leaves: In the small space provided, use a code, such as G for green, YG for yellow-green, DG for dark-green and B for brown.

Many of the pots will have two seedlings, since two seeds were planted. Divide the chart to record data about both seedlings separately; pull out one of the seedlings; or combine the measurements of the two seedlings and record the average. All students should conduct the experiment in the same way.

Growth Chart

Name _____

Chart the growth of one of the measurements you took. Put the data for all three of your pots on one chart. Use different colors or different markings to identify each seedling. Be sure to list which pot and which measurement you're using for each color.

Inches												
5												
4 1/2												
4												
3 1/2												
3												
2 1/2												
2												
1 1/2												
1												
1/2												
Week	1	2	3	4	5	6	7	8	9	10	11	12

2. The Web of Life

Subjects:
Science, Environmental Science, Language Arts, Art

Process Skills:
Listening, reading, using imagination, formulating relationships, stating natural laws

Grades:
3–6

Cognitive Task Level:
Average

Time for Activity:
20 to 30 minutes

Key Vocabulary:
Food web, food chain, interconnected, organism, carnivore, herbivore

Intended Learning Outcomes:
Completing this activity will allow students to:
- Use creativity and imagination to make connections between living things
- Apply ecological concepts in an activity
- Observe the effect of pesticides on the food web.

Background
A food "chain" is a simple chain of organisms eating other organisms, but a food "web" is defined as the network or web of interconnected organisms through which energy is transferred. As energy comes to earth from the sun, it's converted to food energy by plants. All other organisms on earth get their food energy from plants. This food web activity illustrates the interconnectedness of all living things. This concept is especially important with regard to pesticides and fertilizers, whose effects are often subtle and difficult to understand. Learning that all things interact with one another on earth is a good way to start.

Materials
- ❑ Ball of yarn
- ❑ Handouts
  - *Food Web cards*
  - *When The Food Web Gets Out Of Balance*

Procedure
1. Prepare the food web cards. This activity is based on the network of food chains that interact in an ecosystem. Write the names of a full food web on 5-inch x 7-inch cards. To really illustrate the element in the web, glue a representative picture on the card. Attach a string to two ends so that the card can hang around the neck of each student. The cards may also be pinned on the students instead of hanging them. These cards are reusable and can last years.

An example of a typical food web is as follows:

Forest Food Web:
- Sun
- Five plants: Examples include grass, wildflower, poison ivy, oak tree, pine tree, etc.
- Five bugs: Examples include ladybug, dung beetle, bumblebee, wasp, earwig, potato bug, spider, earthworm, butterfly, etc.
- Three reptiles or amphibians: Examples include lizard, frog, snake, turtle, salamander
- Two fish: Examples include trout, salmon, minnows, etc.
- Three songbirds: Examples include robin, mockingbird, sparrow, finch, warbler, blackbird, etc.
- Two raptors: Examples include kestrel, hawk, eagle, kite, vulture, etc.
- Three herbivorous (vegetarian) mammals: Examples include: squirrel, mouse, rabbit, wood rat, deer, elk, antelope, moose, etc.
- Three carnivorous (meat-eating) mammals: Examples include: coyote, badger, raccoon, bobcat, mountain lion, bear, etc.
- Non-living members of the food web that can be added:
  - Water
  - Air
  - Soil

You can add other animals or plants to this food web so that everyone in the class is part of it. You can also reduce the number of animals so that only part of the class actually takes part in the food web while the rest watch.

2. To start this activity, begin a discussion of the food web, or use the handout, When The Food Web Gets Out Of Balance to explain the concept.

3. Hand out food web cards to each student. You may choose to have one big group or use a small group as the example and then divide the class into three groups of eight to ten students.

4. The person who has the Sun card starts the game. The Sun holds the end of the ball of yarn and throws it to someone else in the circle, explaining the connection — "The Sun gives energy to the grass." The next person holds onto the yarn and throws the ball, explaining the connection — "The aphid feeds on the grass."

Each time the yarn is thrown, the individual throwing holds onto his end, so that a web is formed by the yarn in the center of the circle. Examples of other connections include: "The ladybug eats the aphid;" then, "The bird eats the ladybug;" then, "The fruit tree is home to the bird;" then, "The bird is eaten by the hawk." This goes on until everyone holds a piece of the yarn. Make sure the yarn is long enough. The tension on the yarn must be tight to illustrate the interconnectedness of all aspects.

5. Something happens. The teacher points to one individual and announces that this organism is killed due to pesticide. As that plant or animal drops out of the food web and lets go of the yarn, each person who feels the slack of the yarn lets go. Soon, the entire food web has fallen to the ground all because one member of the food chain was killed.

6. This game will be different every time, because animals and plants interact with each other in many different ways. Your students may wish to play this game more than once.

7. Be sure to ask your students what they learned from the game. Ask them what they think would happen if more than one organism in the food web was killed by pesticides. Conversely, what if one organism went out of control? What if there were too many carnivores and very few herbivores? What would the carnivores eat? What might happen to the food web?

Extensions/Modifications

- If you don't have time to find pictures, writing the name of an animal on a card will also work for this activity.

- Pictures of animals can be used to make a food web bulletin board. Have students bring in pictures of plants and animals. Have them use yarn to pin lines to connect the organisms together in a food web. Ask the students to give their reasons for making the connections that they did. The interactions in the food web can change every day, as organisms interact with one another in many different ways.

- This activity can be used by students of all levels, since almost everyone can think of a way to connect the organisms. It's ideal for bilingual classes, as the cards can be written in more than one language or can be used as flashcards for learning English.

When the Food Web Gets Out of Balance

Pelicans and pesticides

The pelican is an important bird in the United States. It occurs on both the eastern and western coasts of North America, and is the state bird of Louisiana. But in the 1970s, pelicans nearly disappeared. At first, scientists were puzzled. Where did all the pelicans go?

They began to watch the pelicans to find out what was happening. They watched the pelicans at their breeding areas. The pelicans laid their eggs, but within a week or two of laying the eggs, all the eggs were broken. This meant that very few pelican chicks were born. This could explain why there were so few pelicans!

But why were the eggs breaking? Was some mysterious predator coming in the middle of the night to break all the eggs? And why would anybody or anything do that? Slowly, scientists guessed that the eggs were simply too thin and they broke when the parents sat on them. Why were the egg shells so delicate?

The scientists collected some broken egg shells and studied them. What they discovered surprised lots of people. The eggshells were thin because the pelicans had high levels of DDT in their systems. But why would the pelicans eat DDT? DDT is a pesticide made for insects, not pelicans. Even more studies traced the DDT to the fish in the ocean. These fish had been exposed to DDT from the runoff of water into the ocean after it had rained.

So, amazing as it sounded, scientists had to conclude that the reason pelican populations were declining was because farmers sprayed DDT on their crops.

The good news is that when farmers stopped using DDT on their crops, the pelican shells got thicker, and more baby pelicans were born. Now we have many pelicans once again.

Questions:
1. Why did scientists decide to study the pelicans?
2. What did scientists find out when they watched the pelicans at their breeding areas?
3. What did the scientists think was the cause of the problem?
4. Where did the DDT come from?
5. What solved the problem of thin-shelled pelican eggs?

What happened on the island of Borneo?

The island of Borneo is a beautiful island that's part of Indonesia. In the 1960s, Borneo had a problem with the disease, malaria, which makes people very sick. Malaria is carried by a type of mosquito.

The officials on Borneo thought that if they could get rid of the mosquito, they could save the islanders from malaria, so they sprayed the island with DDT. This killed the mosquitoes and helped reduce the incidence of malaria. But DDT affected more than just mosquitoes. It also affected other insects, such as roaches and caterpillars.

The geckos (a gecko is a type of lizard) on Borneo like to eat insects. They ate the roaches and caterpillars that had been affected by the DDT. But since geckos eat lots of insects, they got a high concentration of DDT in their system. After awhile, they became slow.

The cats on Borneo liked to eat the geckos. So when the geckos began to move slowly, the cats ate them. But, so much DDT had accumulated in the geckos that when the cats ate the geckos, the cats died.

The cats had also eaten rats that lived in the forests. When the cats died, the rats moved from the forests into the homes of the people. Rats also carry a disease, so the officials of Borneo began to worry about disease all over again.

In order to save the people from the rats, Borneo had to bring in healthy cats that didn't have DDT poisoning. These cats ate the rats, and everything finally seemed to work better.

But there was still one more problem! The people of Borneo lived in grass huts. The roofs of the huts were made of thatch, a type of grass. The caterpillars lived in the thatch on the roofs of the houses and ate the thatch. Normally, the geckos and a species of wasp ate the caterpillars. But the geckos and wasps had been killed by the DDT, so the number of caterpillars grew. The caterpillars ate the thatch roofs until they fell in! The farmers had to build new roofs for their houses.

Questions:
1. Why did the officials of Borneo decide to spray DDT on the island?
2. When the DDT was sprayed, what other animals did it affect but not kill?
3. What happened to the geckos when they ate the roaches and caterpillars?
4. What happened to the cats on Borneo?
5. When the cats died, then what happened?
6. What did the officials of Borneo have to do the stop the rats?
7. What happened to the roofs of Borneo?

Answers to Questions on *When the Food Web Gets Out of Balance* sheet
Answers to Pesticides and pelicans questions:

1 Because their numbers were declining.

2. The eggs of pelicans were breaking when the parents tried to incubate them.

3. They found that DDT was causing the eggs to be thin-shelled and break.

4. The fish that the pelicans ate had DDT in them. The DDT came from runoff after rains.

5. When the use of DDT was stopped, the pelican eggs became stronger and more baby pelicans were born.

Answers to *What happened on the island of Borneo* questions:

1. They were worried about malaria, which is carried by some types of mosquitoes.

2. The roaches and the caterpillars were affected but not outright killed by the poison.

3. They got sick and became slow.

4. The cats ate the lizards and got sick and died.

5. The rats came into the towns and brought the concern of disease.

6. They brought healthy cats in to eat the rats.

7. The caterpillars ate the thatched roofs, causing them to cave in on the people.

3. What Happened to Mr. Johnsons's Fruit Trees?— A Play About Bioaccumulation

Background

Bioaccumulation is a serious concern for wildlife. Some pesticides are stored in the fatty tissues of animals, including people. These toxins can remain in the body for long periods of time. Additional exposure results in further accumulation of the toxin in the body. Since pesticides accumulate in the tissues, in certain instances, pesticide levels increase as if they were being multiplied. This means that very little exposure can lead to serious pesticide poisoning or even death. This is a real danger with certain pesticides. It also makes them difficult to trace because they can be carried long distances in rivers and groundwater systems.

This story offers a simplified version of what can happen in the case of bioaccumulation of a pesticide. In this activity, the teacher or a student reads a story which the other students act out in a play. After the play, math problems help reinforce the concept of the effect of toxin accumulation in the environment. This concept is illustrated well with the transfer of "markers" that represent the pesticide as it travels through the food web. The markers can be any identifier: a sign hung around the neck, a scarf or a hat.

Materials

❏ 16 markers: scarves, signs, name tags, etc.
❏ Handouts:
  - *"What Happened to Mr. Johnson's Fruit Trees?," a play*
  - *Pesticides Pile Up* worksheet

Procedure

1. Assign students to fill the roles of 1 or 2 readers, 1 farmer, 16 insects (8 flies and 8 good bugs), 8 mice, 4 snakes and 2 hawks.

The number of actors can be modified based on class size. Make sure the ratio of insects, mice, snakes and hawks is divisible by two.

2. Have all student actors stand up. As actors finish their roles, have them return to their seats to watch the rest of the play. Distribute several copies of the play, "What Happened to Mr. Johnson's Fruit Trees?" so everyone can read along. Be sure the students know what they're supposed to do when their time comes.

3. Instruct the reader(s) to start reading.

4. After the story is complete, ask the follow-up questions on the teacher's page. Be sure students understand that pesticides are stored in the fatty tissues of the body and they accumulate.

5. After the story, hand out the *Pesticides Pile Up* worksheet to test for comprehension. You may want to go through the worksheet as a class and go over the math problems together.

Extensions/Modification

- Instead of having the entire class participate in the play, you could have only half the class participate while the other half watches. Reduce the numbers of actors accordingly.
- Use the *Pesticides Pile Up* worksheet to test for understanding and as a simple math review.
- This activity works well as a follow-up to the Web of Life activity in this unit. You could have half the class conduct the play, and the other half do the *Web of Life* activity.

Subjects:
Environmental Science, Math, Language Arts

Process Skills:
Reading aloud, acting, addition, multiplication

Grades:
3–6

Cognitive Task Level:
Average to difficult

Time for Activity:
30 minutes

Key Vocabulary:
Insecticide, effects, accumulate, bioaccumulation

Intended Learning Outcomes:
Completing this activity will allow students to:
- Use math problems to understand the cumulative effect of pesticides
- Observe ways pesticides can affect an entire ecosystem
- Gain a greater understanding of the concern raised about pesticides.

What happened to Mr. Johnson's Fruit Trees?

(Stage directions for actors are in italics.)

Mr. Johnson loved his fruit trees. He had a big backyard in the country with apple trees, orange trees, peach trees and lemon trees. One day, he finds his apple trees have been infested with flies that lay their eggs in apples! These eggs hatch into larvae that eat apples. He is horribly upset. He's afraid he won't get any apples from his trees this year.

So Mr. Johnson sprays his trees with insecticide. He doesn't just spray the recommended dose. He overdoes it, thinking that spraying more will ensure he gets his apples. *(Mr. Johnson pretends to spray insecticide on the flies.)* He kills nearly all the flies. *(Eight students who are flies put on insecticide markers.)* He is relieved that he has saved his apples. But, not only does he kill the fly larvae, he also kills ladybugs, praying mantises and honeybees. *(Eight students playing good bugs each put on a marker to represent being killed by pesticide.)*

Now, most mice eat grain. But some mice just love to eat insects. In fact, these mice are a good thing to have around in an orchard. With all the dead and dying insects, the mice eat up the insects. *(Place two markers from the insects on the eight mice.)* But after awhile, the mice don't feel so good. They start to move slowly. Sometimes they stop and go into convulsions. *(Mice act sick.)*

Well, there are four garter snakes in Mr. Johnson's backyard and they're always looking for a meal, so they snap up those sluggish mice. *(Place four markers from the mice onto each of the four snakes.)* But then the snakes start to feel the effects of the toxin and don't move very well at all. *(Snakes act sick.)* In fact, the snakes just stop and lie in the sun.

The hawks feel pretty lucky at finding so much good food in those snakes lying on the ground. *(Place eight markers onto each of the two hawks.)* But, they die from accumulation of the pesticide. *(Hawks die.)*

Epilogue: Mr. Johnson didn't really notice that there were fewer mice, snakes and hawks in his yard, because he was only worried about his apple trees. But the following year, when his orchard should have been buzzing with honeybees, those important insects who pollinate his apple trees, the yard was silent. What happened to the honeybees?

Pesticides Pile Up

Name _____

Now that you've heard the story of Mr. Johnson's apple trees, answer the following mathematics questions.

1. How many insects were there in the story?

2. How many mice were there?

3. How many snakes were there?

4. How many hawks were there?

5. What number can all the numbers be divided by?

Addition or Multiplication

6. What is 2 + 2?

7. What is 2 x 2?

8. Are the results of addition and multiplication the same or different?

9. What is 2 + 2 + 2?

10. What is 2 x 2 x 2?

11. Are the results of addition and multiplication the same or different?

12. What is 2 + 2 + 2 + 2?

13. What is 2 x 2 x 2 x 2?

14. Are the results of addition and multiplication the same or different?

Bioaccumulation

15. How much more insecticide did the mice get than the insects?

16. How much more pesticide did the snakes get than the insects?

17. How much more did the hawks get than the insects?

18. If there had been something that ate the hawks, how much more pesticide would it have gotten than the insects?

19. Based on the math problems above, did the insecticides in this story increase in the environment by addition or by multiplication?

20. Why is over-use of insecticides so dangerous to the ecosystem?

21. Write down some things that you would have told the farmer before he sprayed his trees with insecticide.

What happened in the orchard?

Follow up questions:

1. What happened to the honeybees? They were killed by the pesticide he used to kill the flies.

2. If you knew Mr. Johnson had sprayed his crop of apples with pesticide, how would you feel about eating those apples?

3 Now that you know about the dangers of pesticides, what would you have done if you were Mr. Johnson? If only a small area were infested, he could have picked the larvae off the trees by hand; he could have used smaller quantities of pesticide where the worst infestations occurred. Other options include buying fly-eating insects and releasing them into the trees to eat the flies, or use organic insecticides that target only the problem flies.

Answers to Pesticide Pile-Up Questions

1. 16
2. 8
3. 4
4. 2
5. 2

Addition or Multiplication

6. 4
7. 4
8. They are the same.
9. 6
10. 8
11. Here, the results are different — addition of three 2s is only 6, while multiplication of three 2s is 8.
12. 8
13. 16
14. Here, there is an even greater difference between addition and multiplication. The effects of some pesticides are multiplicative, which means they can accumulate in the body very quickly.

Bioaccumulation

15. Each mouse got two times the amount of pesticide as the insects.
16. The snakes got four times more pesticide.
17. The hawks got eight times more pesticide than the insects.
18. 16 times more insecticide.
19. In this case, by multiplication. The effects of pesticides can multiply at each level of the food chain.
20. If small amounts can kill the problem animals, then what is left over can kill beneficial insects. Also, some insecticides remain in the environment for a long time, killing insects that arrive months later. This is what happened to Mr. Johnson's bees.
21. Examples would include: Be careful how much you use, because the effects can multiply quickly. Instead of spraying the whole orchard, why don't you just spray the badly infested sections? If the problems were concentrated in one zone, you could pick the larvae off by hand. Maybe you should identify a natural insect predator and buy some of them to release in your orchard. I won't eat your apples if you spray them with insecticide. You should tell people to wash those apples before they eat them.

4. The Power of the Pen

Subjects:
Language Arts, Creative Writing, Art

Process Skills:
Listening, synthesizing information, writing poetry, creative visualization

Grades:
4–8

Cognitive Task Level:
Average – Difficult

Time for Activity:
One class period

Key Vocabulary:
Pesticides

Intended Learning Outcomes:
Completing this activity will allow students to:
- Use literature to communicate a message
- Create a poem or story that communicates the student's feelings
- Listen to the words of other writers.

Background
This activity uses writing as a means of powerful communication. Writers use powerful words and eloquent speech to make more than a simple message. Rachel Carson mobilized the entire world with her book, *Silent Spring*, in which she compiled evidence that pesticide use was contributing to mass die-offs of species of plants and animals. In *The Day They Parachuted Cats On Borneo*, Charlotte Pomerantz uses humor, rhyme and fun pictures to educate and inform young people about a serious problem created by pesticides on the island of Borneo.

Materials
- ❏ Introduction to *Silent Spring*, by Rachel Carson
- ❏ *The Day They Parachuted Cats On Borneo*, by Charlotte Pomerantz

Procedure
1. Obtain (from a library or bookstore) one of the books listed in the Materials section above or another book of prose or poetry that transmits an environmental message effectively.

2. Read selected passages. Ask your students if the message actually seems more important because of the way it's written. Explain the value of the written word and its effect on people over time. Note that some writing points to the sadness of loss while other styles use humor to lighten up an issue. Have your students think about what type of message they want to get across.

3. Introduce a method of writing, such as diamante, essay or other poetry so students can develop their use of the written word. You may choose to have your students pick the form they prefer or assign a specific form to them. Adding pictures to illustrate their poems or stories will help.

For instance, a diamante is as follows:

Line 1: One noun
Line 2: Two adjectives
Line 3: Three verbs (using participle form)
Line 4: Four nouns related to nouns in line 1
Line 5: Three verbs related to line 7
Line 6: Two adjectives related to line 7
Line 7: One noun with opposite meaning to line 1 noun

Example:

bugs
ugly, beautiful
munching, creeping, buzzing
butterflies, worms, caterpillars, beetles
growing, caring, helping
supportive, kind
friends

4. After the students have finished their pieces, post them at school where others can see them.

Extensions/Modifications
- Have your students send their poems and stories to their local congressman or senator as part of a letter urging the politician to take action to reduce the threat of pesticides in their community.

Resources for Pesticides and Fertilizers

- *National Pesticide Telecommunications Network*, from Pesticides Hotline: 800-858-7378. Provides help reading the label, information about particular pesticides and emergency information.
- *Healthy Lawn, Healthy Environment: Caring for your Lawn in an Environmentally Friendly Way*, U.S. Environmental Protection Agency, Washington, DC 20460; 202-382-4454.
- *Citizen's Guide to Pesticides*, U.S. Environmental Protection Agency.
- *Western Garden Book*. Sunset Publishing Corporation. Contains information about different methods of pest and disease control, and a wealth of information about gardening.
- *Silent Spring*, by Rachel Carson. Houghton Mifflin Company. This book was the first to point out the dangers of using pesticides.

Books for Students

- *The Day They Parachuted Cats on Borneo*, by Charlotte Pomerantz. Young Scott Books. It is out of print but is still available in many libraries throughout the country.
- *Two Minutes a Day for a Greener Planet*. by Marjorie Lamb. Harper and Row. Includes dozens of ideas that can be used by children or adults to reduce pesticides and other toxic compounds in the home.

Curricula

- *Living Lightly on the Planet*. National Audubon Society. (613 Riversville Road, Greenwich, CT 08630).
- National Arbor Day Foundation, 100 Arbor Avenue, Nebraska City, NE 68410. Materials available include filmstrips, posters, audio cassettes and teacher's guides.
- Soil Conservation Service (SCS), PO Box 2890 Room 6110, Washington, DC 20013. An agency within the U.S. Department of Agriculture which provides leadership in the conservation and use of soil, water and related resources.

Endangered Species

The Challenge

All plants and animals are connected in a complex system called the food web. People, animals and plants share the earth and depend on each other to live. An endangered animal or plant is one that's at risk of becoming extinct. When a species becomes extinct, it disappears from the earth forever. More wildlife is endangered now than ever before.

Every step to help endangered species helps us all to survive because we all fit into the food web.

Did You Know?

- Today, more than 200 animal species in the United States are endangered. Worldwide, it's even scarier. More than 1,000 animals are endangered. As many as ten species disappear every day.
- Little-noticed water animals are in big trouble. In North America, a third of our fish species, two-thirds of our crayfish species and nearly three-quarters of the mussel species are in trouble.
- Why are they dying? The causes of the extinction of most species

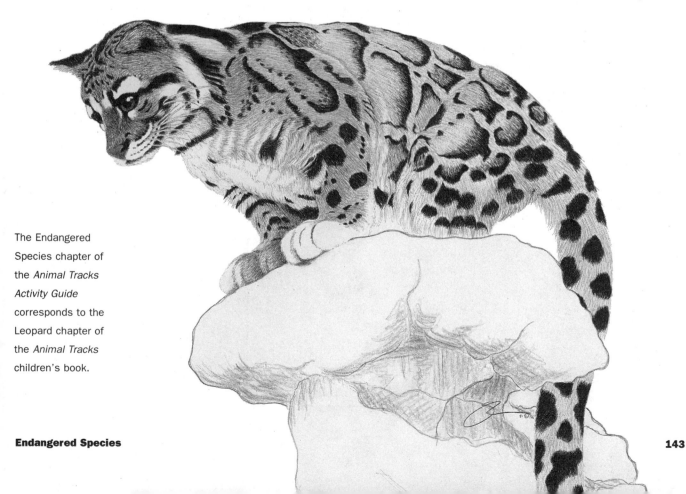

The Endangered Species chapter of the *Animal Tracks Activity Guide* corresponds to the Leopard chapter of the *Animal Tracks* children's book.

fall into the following categories: loss of habitat due to human development; over-hunting, including illegal trading of animal furs, feathers and other parts; and pollution caused by oil spills, acid rain and pesticide poisoning.

- In 1973, the U.S. Congress passed the Endangered Species Act. It said no "threatened" (likely to become endangered in the near future) or "endangered" species can be imported, exported, killed, owned, bought, sold or taken from the wild without a special permit. The law also protects the habitats of endangered and threatened species. It's been so successful that the California gray whale, bald eagle, peregrine falcon and American alligator are no longer in danger of extinction.

- We can't rely on the government to do it all. Land conservation programs set aside unspoiled wilderness to shelter animals and plants and protect their habitats. That helps conserve, or save, the natural diversity, or variety of life, on our planet.

- People can help too. One way to preserve a species is to improve habitat for animals. A bird box where it's needed, a restored wetland, a planted tree all contribute to improving habitat.

1. Where in the World?

Subjects:
Social Studies, Geography, Language Arts

Process Skills:
Reading, locating places, writing

Grades:
3–6

Cognitive Task Level:
Simple to average

Time for Activity:
15 to 20 minutes of homework, then 5 to 10 minutes in class

Key Vocabulary:
Endangered, extinct, habitat, organism, species

Intended Learning Outcomes:
Completing this activity will allow students to:
- Gain experience locating places on a map
- Learn about endangered species
- Write a brief description of the species to share with others.

Background

An endangered species is a plant or animal in danger of becoming extinct. Signals that an animal may be approaching extinction and should be considered endangered include a decline in the number of individuals of that species, a significant loss of habitat or a reduction in the number of offspring produced. Plants and animals throughout the world are becoming endangered and extinct.

Your students can broaden their horizons and learn about other parts of the world by conducting a little research on endangered species. This activity involves learning about endangered species of plants and animals, then selecting a species, bringing a picture of it with a brief description to class and indicating its location on a world map. Cutting pictures of endangered species from old magazines will make this a more colorful activity. Since these descriptions are relatively easy to do, you may want to give extra credit points to students who bring in more than one.

Materials
- ❑ Large world map on a large bulletin board
- ❑ Yarn or string
- ❑ Pushpins
- ❑ Pictures of endangered species with a brief description (as an example)
- ❑ Books or magazines about endangered species.

Procedure

1. Introduce the subject of endangered species to your students. Most students are familiar with the term but may not understand what it means. Point out that many human activities are the cause of the increase in endangered species. To make your example, cut out a picture of an endangered species from a magazine, or photocopy a picture of one from a book and include information beneath it, like the name of the organism, where it occurs, what type of habitat it lives in and causes of endangerment.

Your example might look something like this:

- Name of Organism: California Condor
- Where It Occurs: Southern California, USA
- What type of habitat it lives in: Grasslands
- Causes of endangerment: Hunting, habitat destruction, poison traps

2. Show your example to your students. Explain to your students the difference between the geographic location of a species — for example, Australia, or Southern California — and its habitat (rainforest, desert, stream, grasslands, etc.).

3. Using pushpins and string, pin your example near the map and place the string so that it creates a line pointing to the geographic location of the organism. In the case of this example, the line would point to southern California.

4. Have your students make their own endangered species descriptions as a homework assignment. Encourage students to bring in examples of both animals and plants. For students who need help getting started, let them look through old magazines. This activity provides a great opportunity to use old issues of magazines such as National Geographic or International Wildlife. If a student finds a picture in a book, simply photocopying the picture will work.

5. When students bring their endangered species descriptions to class, help them locate the correct geographic location on the world map.

Extensions/Modifications

- To make the descriptions appear neater, require that they be typed. This can facilitate use of the typewriter or computer. To practice handwriting skills, have the students write their descriptions by hand.

- To broaden this activity, simply have students find pictures of any animal or plant and follow the same procedure. This emphasizes the geography and does not address the endangered species issue at all.

- Have students contact a local, state, national or international organization that offers animal "adoption." In exchange for an "adoption" fee, recipients receive regular updates on an individual's status. The fee is often used to promote habitat conservation.

2. How Biologists Learn About Animals

Subjects:
Science, Geography, Math, Language Arts

Process Skills:
Reading directions, plotting points, measuring distances, determining averages.

Grades:
4–6

Cognitive Task Level:
Average to difficult

Time for Activity:
20 to 30 minutes

Key Vocabulary:
Biologist, coniferous forest, range, territory

Intended Learning Outcomes:
Completing this activity will allow students to:
- Develop skills that biologists use for tracking animals
- Calculate distances between nesting sites of bald eagles
- Predict the next nest site based on what they learned.

Background
Biologists learn about animals by watching them and by learning their habits and behaviors. Biologists can't preserve animal populations if they don't know what they need to survive. This activity simulates a method that was used by biologists in the 1950s, before bald eagles became endangered. It allowed biologists to find out the amount of habitat a pair of eagles needed in order to raise their chicks. The amount of area that an animal uses daily is called its range. The range of an animal differs in different areas, depending on the availability of food and the intensity of competition with other members of the same species.

This type of information was useful for biologists after the numbers of bald eagles dropped in the 1960s and 1970s. As part of the recovery program, biologists were able to release captive-born eagles into areas with plenty of suitable habitat. They knew how many eagles they could release into one particular area without over-populating it. This is just one reason why it's important to understand how animals function in the wild.

Materials
- ❏ Rulers
- ❏ Compasses
- ❏ Pencils and erasers
- ❏ Calculators (optional)
- ❏ Handouts
  - *Where Is The Eagle's Nest?*
  - *Eagle Lake Area Map*

Procedure
1. Have your students work in groups of three. Each group needs a ruler, a pencil and eraser, calculator and a compass.

2. Distribute the Eagle Lake Area Map and Where Is The Eagle's Nest? Have the students follow the story on the handout. Have them plot the points where eagle nests were observed. After the points are marked on the map, they must measure the distance from one nest to the next. They then average the distances between nests.

3. Using nest 3 as the last nest observed, students must calculate where the next nest should occur.

4. The teacher's version of the handout has the answer to the location of nest 4. Have students check their answers with the teacher. Enthusiastic students can locate other nests. These are also noted on the teacher's version.

5. Ask your students to come up with ideas on other ways they can use these methods to learn about animals.

Extensions/Modifications
- Invite a biologist to come to the classroom and describe other ways that biologists study animals.
- Apply some of these methods to learn about animals in real life. See the "Squirrel Chapter" for more ideas.

Where Is The Eagle's Nest?

Name _____

You're a biologist working in the coniferous forests of the Pacific Northwest. Your job is to determine the population of nesting bald eagles around Eagle Lake. Even though bald eagles have been removed from the federal list of Endangered Species, their numbers must still be monitored closely to make sure they are breeding successfully in the wild.

Look at the map of the area around Eagle Lake. Someone in the area reported seeing an eagle's nest from the old highway. This nest is marked on the map. Label this nest "Nest 1." Hiking along the lake, you find another eagle's nest! This nest is 20 miles due east of Nest 1. Using your ruler and a scale of 1 inch = 5 miles, mark Nest 2 on your map.

One week later, as you are hiking through the forest, you find another nest! This nest is northeast of Nest 1. To locate this nest on your map, go 10 miles east and 20 miles north from Nest 1. Mark Nest 3 on the map.

It took a long time to locate these three nests. To survey the entire area on foot will take much longer, and the nesting season may be over before you finish. You must find a way to look for the eagle nests that takes less time.

Take your compass or ruler and measure the distance from Nest 1 to Nest 2. Then, measure the distance between Nest 2 and Nest 3. Then measure the distance between Nest 1 and Nest 3. Write the answers below.

Distance between Nest 1 and Nest 2:

Distance between Nest 2 and Nest 3:

Distance between Nest 1 and Nest 3:

Find the average distance between the three nests by adding up all three distances and divide by 3. Write the average distance between the three nests here _____

It isn't a coincidence that the distance between the three nests is about the same. Like most birds, when eagles raise young, they must forage each day for food to feed their chicks. If two eagles hunt in the same area, they compete with each other for food. To avoid this competition, eagles establish a range, or territory, that they use to hunt for food. Other eagles who enter this territory are chased away. When there are two eagles' nests, the eagles will split the distance between the two nests.

Set your compass to the average distance between nests. Then place the point of your compass on Nest 2. Draw a circle around it. Then set your compass point to nest 3. Draw a circle around that. Where the two circles meet is the most likely place for the next nest to be. To double check your calculations, use your ruler to measure the distance from Nests 2 and 3 to the new nest site. Is it about the same as the distance between the other nests? _____

Your teacher knows about where the next nest site is located. Check with your teacher to see if you correctly predicted where the next nest site will be. Using this method of prediction, you will be able to find other eagle nests much more quickly. Use what you learned to find any other nests sites on the map.

Map of Eagle Lake

Name

Old Highway

Nest #1

Eagle Lake

N
W   E
S

Scale
1" = 5 miles

Map of Eagle Lake
(Teacher's Version)

Teacher's Version

Nest #4

Nest #3

Nest #2

Nest #1

Old Highway

Eagle Lake

N
W   E
S

Scale
1" = 5 miles

3. Animal "Spirit" Masks

Subjects:
Social Studies, Language
Arts, Art

Process Skills:
Describing characteristics,
creating models, writing
descriptions

Grades:
3–6

Cognitive Task Level:
Average

Time for Activity:
Two to four 50-minute
class periods

Key Vocabulary:
Spirit, qualities, papier mâché

**Intended Learning
Outcomes:**
Completing this activity will
allow students to:

• Develop a positive feeling
  towards animals
• Design and make a papier
  mâché animal mask
• Discuss the role animals
  have in everyday society.

Background

In earlier eras, many cultures identified closely with the plants and animals they saw and hunted. They would draw pictures of them, build totem poles or make elaborate headdresses depicting these animals. Sometimes, they would pretend they were these animals and would imagine they had the animal's "spirit." These people hoped they would acquire the strength, power, wisdom or other qualities of the animals they imitated.

Even today, some people will keep a piece of an animal with them — a lucky rabbit's foot, a bear claw or a bird's feather. It's almost as if keeping these things gives them special strengths that will make them more successful in life. Instead of carrying a piece of a real animal for luck or strength, we can achieve some of the same value from photographing or making a piece of art about an animal.

The purpose of this activity is to reinforce the importance of animals in our world. Students think about an animal that they admire, then make a "spirit mask" of that animal. As they make their masks they should think of the animal they have chosen and the qualities it possesses that they admire. When finished, these masks may carry some of the "spirit" that went into their making.

Materials
❑ Several bottles of starch
    or
    ❑ 1 5-pound bag of flour
    ❑ salt
    ❑ water

❑ Newspaper
❑ Florist's wire or any bendable,
    cuttable wire
❑ Scissors
❑ Non-toxic, water-based
    glossy paint
❑ Reusable dishes for the starch
    mixture
❑ Molds for heads: A used gallon
    milk jug, inverted, works well.
    Other molds include balloons,
    polystyrene head molds or
    inexpensive face masks
❑ 3-inch x 5-inch cards

Procedure

1. First, talk about animals with your students. Ask them to think of a favorite animal and describe it. As the students describe animals, write the name of the animal and the descriptive words on the board or have your students write them down on a piece of paper. For example:

BEAR: Big, strong, smart, lives in forests

FROG: Lives near water, makes nice sounds at night, green

Your students also may have some poetic ideas about animals. For example:

LION: Noble, proud, fast, ferocious, wise, and loyal

Encourage your students to be creative with their descriptions. For ideas, refer to the animals used in the *Animal Tracks* book and the introduction to each unit of this *Activities Guide*.

2. After they understand the concept as a class, instruct each student to select an animal they admire. Have them write down the name of that animal and several qualities they admire. You can have them do this as a homework assignment and instruct them to bring in a picture of that animal to the next class. If this part of the activity is done in class, have books with pictures of animals available to help them get ideas of the appearance of the animals they select.

3. When everyone has selected an animal, instruct them on how to make a papier mâché mask. An excellent mask mold is the gallon-sized plastic milk jug. To make it into a mask mold, follow the instructions on the following page. Use the florist's wire to add antlers, ears or whiskers. Assist your students as they create a mold of their animal with the milk jug and wire. The plastic milk jug can be cut and hole-punched. Help students who need to attach antlers or ear-shaped pieces of wire.

4. To make the starch mixture, mix 1 cup of starch with 1/2 cup of water. To use the flour, salt and water mixture, use one cup flour to 1/2 cup salt and add water to create a consistency of thin yogurt. Distribute several dishes of the mixture so that everyone can reach a dish easily. Have your students tear the newspaper into strips about 1 inch wide.

5. Your students place newspaper strips dipped in the starch or flour mixture over their molds. After dipping each piece of newspaper, students wipe excess with their fingers so that each piece of paper is lightly coated with the papier mâché mixture. Place a little extra newspaper over weak spots on the mold. After the molds are covered with papier mâché, leave them out to dry completely. This may take one or two days.

6. After the molds have dried, they can be painted to look like the animals they are supposed to be. Help your students mix colors.

7. Have your students write on a 3-inch x 5-inch card what their spirit animal is and what qualities it possesses that the student admires. Mount the heads on the classroom wall with the cards placed underneath them.

Extensions/Modifications

- This activity can use any type of animal or be limited to endangered species. To expand it, have your students conduct a short research report about the animal they select, including where it's found, how many remain in the world, whether it's considered endangered and what's being done to protect it. Include these one-page reports below the animal masks.

- This activity can be simplified by simply making it a writing and drawing activity. Have your students write down the qualities of the animal they select and either draw a picture or paste a picture of the animal next to the text.

Instruction for Using a Gallon Milk Jug for Mask Making

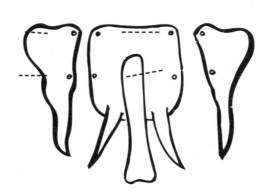

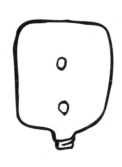
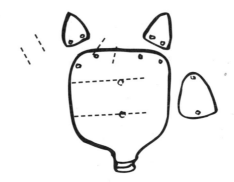

4. Animal Tracks - Review Words and Concepts

Subjects:
Social Studies, Language Arts

Process Skills:
Reading, writing, deciphering clues

Grades:
3–6

Cognitive Task Level:
Average

Time for Activity:
20 minutes

Intended Learning Outcomes:
Completing this activity will allow students to:
- Develop vocabulary words relating to endangered species and their habitats
- Learn some of the common causes that lead to endangerment
- Review some of the concepts learned in previous chapters

Background
This word fill-in and word scramble offers a chance to sum up the concepts presented in this chapter and other chapters of the Animal Tracks book and the Activities Guide. You can use it as a way to check for understanding and comprehension. The words in the Word Scramble are the same as those used in the Fill-in. You can assign the Fill-in as a test and have the students find the words later in the Word Scramble, or just use the two activities as a fun way to wrap up the unit.

Materials
- Teacher's Page
- Handouts
    - *Fill-In*
    - *Word Scramble*

Procedure
1. To use as a test for comprehension, hand out the Fill-In and grade the student's answers. For an easier version, hand out the Word Scramble and let the students find the words first, then use them to fill in the blanks in the Fill-In.

2. Use the activity to start a discussion on what your students have learned and how they plan to use their knowledge in the future.

Word Fill-In

Name _____

1. An animal's _____ is its home.

2. The clouded leopard lives in the tropical _____ of India and southern Asia. It is endangered mainly because its home is being converted into farmland.

3. This type of habitat is very dry. Animals that live here are masters at conserving water and staying cool._____

4. The Snow Leopard lives in the _____ of China and Tibet. It is endangered partly because it is hunted for its beautiful fur.

5. DDT, a type of _____ , once caused many species of birds to become endangered, including the bald eagle, brown pelican and peregrine falcon. They have all recovered since DDT was banned.

6. Humans have always hunted animals, but _____ can cause problems for some species of animals.

7. Acid _____ has killed some fish and frogs in the Great Lakes Region of the United States. It is caused by air pollution.

8. Destroying an animal's habitat can cause it to become _____ .

9. _____ learn about animals by observing them, counting them, and tracking them.

10. This great bird is the symbol of America. It was once endangered because of hunting and pesticide poisoning, but it is now making a spectacular comeback. _____
   _____ .

11. Everyone can help animals by creating good habitat in their own
   _____ .

12. _____ are places where animals are kept and protected.

13. You can help your local zoo or nature center by becoming a
   _____ .

14. By preserving as many different types of plants, animals, and habitats as possible, we are preserving _____ .

15. Some habitat is destroyed to build dams or power plants. By conserving _____ we can avoid building more power plants.

16. _____ saves habitats too — when we use things over again, we don't need to use so many natural resources.

17. Clean _____ is a requirement for all living things. Don't dump garbage into lakes or rivers!

18. By using non-toxic household products, we reduce the chance of causing
   _____

19. Recycling _____ helps save trees.

20. The secrets to saving wildlife are in following animal _____ .

Animal Tracks Activity Guide

Word Scramble

Name _____

```
E B A L D E A G L E X M Y P
O B I O L O G I S T S O A E
V O L U N T E E R R X U B S
E P Q E R B B T G A P N I T
R A O X N Z A L M C H T Y I
H P R L F D S C R K X A G C
U E W E L R A T K S Y I R I
N R S S D U W N T Y F N E D
T G T H J A T R G K A S N E
I L S Z T C E I V E B R E N
N M E E G S T V O W R X D X
G Z R Q E S D F G N X E X S
B I O D I V E R S I T Y D O
H J F R E C Y C L I N G R O
H A B I T A T R A I N W P Z
```

Words to find:

habitat	endangered	energy
forests	biologists	recycling
deserts	bald eagle	water
mountains	backyards	pollution
pesticide	zoos	paper
overhunting	volunteer	tracks
rain	biodiversity	

Teacher's Page
Answers to *Word Fill-In*

1. habitat
2. forests
3. deserts
4. mountains
5. pesticide
6. overhunting
7. rain
8. endangered
9. biologists
10. bald eagle
11. backyards
12. zoos
13. volunteer
14. biodiversity
15. energy
16. recycling
17. water
18. pollution
19. paper
20. tracks

Answers to Word Scramble

```
E B A L D E A G L E X M Y P
O B I O L O G I S T S O A E
V O L U N T E E R R X U B S
E P Q E R B B T G A P N I T
R A O X N Z A L M C H T Y I
H P R L F D S C R K X A G C
U E W E L R A T K S Y I R I
N R S S D U W N T Y F N E D
T G T H I A T R G K A S N E
I L S Z T C E I V E B R E N
N M E E G S T V O W R X D X
G Z R Q E S D F G N X E X S
B I O D I V E R S I T Y D O
H J F R E C Y C L I N G R O
H A B I T A T R A I N W P Z
```

Resources for Endangered Species

Books for Students

- *Will We Miss Them?*, by Alexandra Wright. Charlesbridge Publishing Co. An excellent book about some endangered species, with illustrations of the animals and their habitats.

- *Smart Survivors, Twelve of the Earth's most remarkable Living Things*, by Sneed B. Collard, III. NorthWord Press, Inc. An interesting book that addresses animals that have developed unique adaptations for survival. Covers more than endangered animals.

- *Endangered Habitats*, by Jenny Tesar. Part of the Our Fragile Planet Series, Facts On File Press. Includes photographs of animals and descriptions of habitats.

Books for Adults

- *The Diversity of Life*, by E.O. Wilson, W.W. Norton & Co. This excellent book provides a challenging argument in favor of preserving biodiversity.

General

- *The Atlas of Endangered Species*, edited by John Burton. MacMillan Publishing Co. A beautiful book of photographs and descriptions of habitats.

- *Witness: Endangered Species of North America*, by Susan Middleton and David Liittschwager. Chronicle Books. A beautiful photo essay that describes the species, its present population and the greatest threat to its survival.

Education Materials

- *Ranger Rick's Nature Scope: Endangered Species: Wild and Rare*. National Wildlife Federation. A thorough overview of the causes for endangerment with many thought-provoking activities.

Glossary

accumulate — to collect or gather.

actinomycetes — a type of microorganism found in soil. They decompose organic matter in compost piles.

ad campaign — a planned action to inform the public about an event that is broadcast through different forms of media, such as television, radio or newspapers.

additive — produced by addition. Additive effects increase more slowly that multiplicative effects.

aerate — exposing something to air. In composting, aeration provides an aerobic environment for decomposer organisms. Air is needed to change minerals into forms that are usable by plants.

aluminum — A bluish, silver-white light metal that can be bent or crushed easily. It is highly resistant to rust.

aquatic life — organisms that live and grow in water

aquifer — a natural area that holds and stores water for drinking wells.

atmosphere — the envelope of gases that surround the earth.

bacteria — single-celled living organisms, some of which help to break down solid waste.

bauxite — the principal ore of aluminum.

benthic — the bottom of a body of water. The benthic region is on the ocean or lake floor.

bioaccumulation — to collect a substance, in the body or in an ecosystem, for a period of time. Bioaccumulation usually refers to collection of toxic substances in the body which eventually overcome the body's ability to function, thus killing it.

biologist — a person who studies nature. "bio" = life, "ology" = study of.

biotic assessment — a study and catalog of all life in a given area. A biotic assessment typically includes a list of all the plants and animals that occur in an area.

captive breeding — a program used in zoos to increase the population of endangered species of animals.

carnivore — an animal that eats other animals.

cast — something formed from a material that is poured into a mold. Casts are made of animal tracks and other things.

chemical — a substance made by man or nature which is composed of molecules, which are atoms that are joined together. Atoms are the basic unit of matter. Chemicals are created by people to help make thousands of useful products. But when chemicals get into our environment, they can cause sickness, injury, or death to wildlife and people.

chlorinate — to add chlorine. Chlorination is used in water treatment to kill bacteria and other microorganisms that occur in water.

coagulation — to change from a fluid to a thickened mass; to clump smaller aggregates into larger ones.

commercial — paid advertising or promotional announcement.

compassion — a feeling of deep sympathy for another.

compost — organic material that has decomposed into a dark, earth-smelling humus-like material. In biological decomposition of organic materials by microorganisms, compost is the soil-like product.

compromise — a settlement of difference between two parties that often involves each party conceding a part.

condensation — the change of vapor or a gas into a liquid, normally caused by cooling.

conference — a meeting of several individuals to discuss a topic.

coniferous forest — a forest composed almost entirely of evergreen trees, like pine trees. Large expanses of coniferous forests occur in the Pacific Northwest of the United States.

consideration — careful thought or deliberation

conservation — planned management of a natural resource to prevent exploitation, destruction or neglect.

consumption — the use of economic goods in the satisfaction of wants or in the process of production resulting chiefly in their destruction, deterioration or transformation.

containment — the act of holding within a certain area.

contaminant — a substance that taints another substance; something that does not belong.

continent — one of the earth's largest continuous units of landmass. The earth's continents include Eurasia (often considered from a historical point of view as two separate continents, Europe and Asia), Africa, North America, South America, Antarctica and Australia.

create — to produce or make.

creature — an animal.

current — a large portion of air or water moving in the same direction.

decomposer — an organism that assists in the breakdown of materials.

detergent — chemical used as a substitute for soap. There are many kinds of detergent, some much stronger than soap.

decision — the act of making up one's mind.

decompose — to decay, rot, come apart or break down into simpler components.

dichotomous key — di-chot = two parts. A guide to identifying organisms that offers only two options at each step of the guide. This system was designed by Linnaeus in the 1700s and is widely used by scientists to this day.

digest — when food particles are softened by chemicals in the stomach and digestive tract so that nutrients can be absorbed into the body.

distribution — the act of giving out or spreading around a material or product.

drought — an extended period of dry weather.

economics — the study of the manufacture, production and consumption of goods and services.

effect — a result that is produced by an action or event.

efficiency — functioning in the least wasteful manner.

empathy — identifying with the feelings or needs of another.

endangered — a plant or animal that is in danger of becoming extinct.

energy — the ability to do work. Energy is what makes our bodies run and machines work. Energy occurs in different forms, including chemical energy and physical energy. Burning fossil fuels generates energy, as does falling water and windmills. These types of energy are harnessed to do work.

enhance — to improve.

environment — All the conditions, circumstances and influences surrounding and affecting the development or existence of people or nature.

erosion — the loss of topsoil due to excessive water run-off.

evaporation — the change of the state of a liquid to a gas or vapor.

extinct — no living members of the species exist.

faucet — a device that controls the flow of water through a pipe.

fertilizer — a substance used to add nutrients to the soil. Fertilizers can be organic, such as compost and manure, or inorganic, produced by chemical processes in a laboratory.

filtration — to pass a liquid through a substance that traps impurities.

food chain — the interrelationship of a series of organisms in an ecosystem. Each organism feeds on the previous organisms in the food chain. Example: grass > mouse > snake > hawk.

food web — complex relationship formed by interconnecting and overlapping food chains.

force — physical strength or influence.

fossil fuels — fuels formed from the remains of plants and animals that lived long ago. Petroleum and coal are examples of fossil fuels.

fund-raiser — an event whose purpose is to collect money for a cause or charity.

fungus — a class of organisms that have no chlorophyll. Examples are yeasts, molds and mushrooms. Their feeding processes cause decomposition of organic matter (parasitic). Plural: fungi.

gas — a mist-like substance whose molecules are light enough to remain suspended in air.

garbage — any material considered worthless, offensive or unnecessary and is thrown away.

gaseous — a substance suspended in air.

glacier — a large mass of ice formed from snow that moves slowly through mountains.

glass — a hard, brittle, non-chrystalline substance created by fusing silica, soda ash and lime at a temperature of approximately 2700° Fahrenheit.

gravity — the force of attraction directed on items that draws them downward (toward the center of the earth.)

groundwater — water stored beneath the earth's surface in porous rock and soils. More than half of the United States water supply comes from groundwater.

growth — the process of increasing in size by natural development.

habit — customary use or practice.

habitat — the place where an organism or community of organisms lives

height — the distance between the lowest and highest points of an individual or organism.

herbivore — animals that eat only plants.

humus — dark, spongy, earthy-smelling material resulting from partial decomposition of plant or animal matter that forms the organic portion of soil.

hydroelectric — the energy produced by moving water. This includes falling streams and tidal movements. It is used to generate electric power.

hydrologic cycle — the water cycle, composed of the four stages: evaporation, condensation, precipitation, and accumulation.

imagine — to form a mental image of something not actually present.

indigestible — something that can't be broken down by the body's own chemicals. Indigestible items are ejected by the body either by regurgitation or by excretion.

indoor air pollution — particulates and toxic materials produced by articles that occur indoors. The fumes generated from a new carpet are a form of indoor air pollution.

interest group — a group of individuals who all support a common interest.

insecticide — a chemical substance that kills insects.

invertebrate — an animal that has no backbone. Crustaceans, arthropods and earthworms are examples of invertebrates.

jingle — a short, repetitive song; jingles are often used in advertising.

jojoba — a type of bean that produces a fine oil. This oil can be used for fuel and lubrication purposes.

landfill — facility where solid waste is disposed of by spreading it in layers and covering it with soil.

litter — carelessly discarded trash, waste paper or garbage.

macroorganism — a living thing large enough to be seen with the human eye. Examples include decomposers such as worms, ants, snails, pincher bugs, millipedes, spiders or beetles.

manufacturing plant — a facility where the making of goods or wares on a large scale occurs.

materials recovery facility — a facility where items that have been collected from recycling programs, like aluminum cans or glass bottles, are collected, sorted and prepared for shipping.

media — means of communication that reaches large groups of people, such as television, radio or newspapers.

mesosphere — the region of the earth's atmosphere between the stratosphere and the thermosphere.

metric — the standard of measurement commonly used in Europe whose main unit of measurement is the meter, not the foot.

microorganism — a living thing unable to be seen with the naked eye. Examples include some fungi, yeasts, molds and bacteria. Many decomposers are microorganisms.

multiplicative — an increase in number that occurs from multiplying the starting numbers instead of adding them. A multiplicative increase is one that increases very rapidly.

native — an original inhabitant of a region or country. Native plants are plants that have always existed in an area and have not been introduced.

natural resources — the natural wealth of a country, consisting of land, forests, mineral deposits, water, etc.

negative cast — when making animal track casts, a negative cast is created by making a second cast from a positive cast.

nuclear — form of energy in which a chain reaction in a radioactive fuel is maintained and controlled to produce heat.

open space — an area left undisturbed for the enjoyment of people and other living things.

ore — a type of rock that contains metal.

organism — a living thing

organic — made from living organisms, such as plants and animals

ozone — a form of oxygen. The ozone layer is a protective layer of ozone high in the earth's atmosphere that filters out much of the sun's harmful ultraviolet radiation. The ozone hole is the thinning of the ozone layer caused by the release of chlorine atoms from chemicals such as CFCs. Low-level ozone is the main ingredient of smog and is found near ground level.

packaging — the act, art, industry, process or style of packing; containing a bundle of similar or identical items.

paper — A substance made from wood fibers or other fibrous material, usually in thin sheets, used for writing, printing or wrapping things.

papier mâché — a substance made of paper pulp mixed with glue and used to shape articles; it hardens when dry.

particles — very small bits of matter that become suspended in air.

percentage — a rate or proportion per hundred.

pesticide — a substance used to kill pests, such as insects or weeds.

petroleum — an oily, thick, flammable liquid, usually dark-colored, that is a mixture of various hydrocarbons, occurring naturally in various parts of the world and commonly obtained by drilling.

permeability — the speed at which water or some other liquid passes through a substrate.

pH — the level of acidity and alkalinity in a substance. Neutral pH is measured at 7.0 . Levels of pH lower than 7.0 indicate higher amounts of acidity and levels of pH greater than 7.0 indicate higher levels of alkalinity. These measurements of acidity and alkalinity can be made with a special type of paper and with certain chemicals. Acidity and alkalinity can influence the type of vegetation that is able to grow in the soil.

plaster of Paris — a white powder made of gypsum that hardens quickly when mixed with water. It is used for making casts and molds.

plastic — refers to a group of materials, composed mostly of petroleum byproducts, that may be shaped when soft and then hardens. Early plastics were made from organic materials.

pollutants — harmful substances deposited in the air, water or on land, leading to a state of dirtiness, impurity or unhealthiness.

pollution — a human-caused change in the physical, chemical, or biological conditions of the environment that creates an undesirable effect on living things.

positive cast — when making animal casts, a positive cast is one that has the cast of the print projecting outward from the casting.

precipitation — the process of condensing from moisture and falling to earth as rain or snow.

prevailing winds — winds that consistently blow in one direction. The trade winds and the westerly winds are prevailing winds.

pulp — moist fiber materials from which paper and paperboard are made.

qualities — features or characteristics of a person, place or thing.

range — the area that an animal will travel to forage for food.

recycle — to pass through or undergo again, as for further treatment, change or use.

recycling center — a site where manufactured materials are collected and resold for reprocessing.

refuse — something that is discarded as worthless or useless.

replace — to provide a substitute in the place of something.

reuse — to extend the life of an item by using it again and again in its same form; repairing an item, modifying it or creating a new use for it.

reservoir — a place where water is stored.

run-off — water that is not absorbed into the soil.

sedimentation — the process in which loose solid matter settles to the bottom; the heaviest matter settles first; the lightest materials settle out last.

sewage treatment system — a complex system that collects and transports waste water, purifies it and ultimately releases it.

sewers — an underground pipeline that transports waste water and refuse.

steam — the vaporous state of water. Water turns to steam when the temperature is increased.

steel — a modified form of iron that is artificially produced. It has carbon content higher than wrought iron and lower than pig iron. Steel is magnetic.

solar energy — energy obtained directly from the sun, through the use of plate collectors, reflecting mirrors or other devices

source — the origin of something; a spring is the source of a stream or river, a mineral deposit is a source of a natural resource.

source reduction — Any efforts that are made to reduce the amount, quantity or toxicity of materials before they enter the garbage can.

species — distinct individuals of a population that can interbreed with one another.

spirit — the essence of a character, human or animal. It represents the part of the character that does not exist in the body.

steam — the vaporous state of water. Water turns to steam when the temperature is increased above its boiling point.

storyboard — A poster that tells a story or augments a story told by someone else.

stratosphere — the atmospheric layer that occurs 7 to 15 miles above the earth, immediately above the troposphere.

survival — the ability to stay alive in the face of difficult circumstances.

terrarium — a glass box where small plants and animals are kept.

territory — an area of land owned or supervised by one individual. In wildlife terms, a territory is the area that an animal actively defends.

thermosphere — The highest, thinnest, outer layer of the atmosphere. 99 percent of all air occurs below this layer.

threatened — plants and animals that are in danger of becoming extinct. Their situation is not as immediate as plants and animals that are considered endangered, but without intervention, the organisms will most likely become endangered.

tracks — the footprints of an animal

trade winds — prevailing winds that blow in an easterly direction along the equator.

troposphere — the atmospheric layer closest to the earth. Most storms and clouds occur in this sphere.

toxic — substance containing poison and posing a substantial threat to human health and/or the environment.

vapor — the gaseous state of a liquid. Steam is water vapor.

vermicomposting — composting with worms (vermus is Latin for worm).

volume — amount of space, measured in cubic units, that an object or substance occupies.

waste — anything which is discarded; a by—product which may have reusable or recyclable contents.

waterway — a body of water that is used for transportation. Canals and rivers are examples of waterways.

weight — amount, quantity of heaviness or mass that a given object possesses.

westerly winds — prevailing winds that blow in a westerly direction. They occur both to the north and to the south of the equator.

wildlife — animals living in nature

windmill — a machine driven by the wind blowing against blades or shafts. Windmills convert wind energy into mechanical or electrical energy.

Notes

Order Form

The Animal Tracks conservation education program:
- *Animal Tracks Activity Guide* available from the NEA Professional Library (1-800-229-4200)
- *Animal Tracks On-Line*, a new interactive resource on the Internet's World Wide Web
- *Animal Tracks*, the companion book for children, available from the NWF (1-800-432-6564)

Animal Tracks Activity Guide:

Call or write the NEA Professional Library and ask for Stock # 1872-9-00-C4. The price per book is $9.95 (plus $3.50 shipping and handling per book.) Please include CA or DC sales tax if applicable.

NEA Professional Library, P.O. Box 509, West Haven, CT 06516-9904.   1-800-229-4200

Animal Tracks On-Line:

A new on-line educational resource with environmental information and activities for classroom use.
Check us out on the World Wide Web at http://www.nwf.org/nwf

Animal Tracks Children's Book: **Source 505698**

To order, call NWF at 1-800-432-6564 or mail a copy of this form to:
National Wildlife Federation, 1400 16th Street NW, Washington, D.C. 20036-2266

Name: _____

Address_____

_____

City _____State _____Zip Code _____

In case we have questions about your order:
Daytime telephone: _____

Method of payment:
❏ My check is enclosed (made payable to **National Wildlife Federation**)
❏ My school's purchase order #_____ is enclosed.
❏ Please charge my Visa, MasterCard or Discover

Account #_____-_____-_____-_____

Authorized signature:_____Expiration date:_____

Call toll free 1-800-432-6564

Item	Item#	Quantity	Price Each	Total Amount
Animal Tracks book	79929		$5.00	
Order 30 or more books and receive a 30% discount	79929-3		$3.30	
			SUBTOTAL:	
			Plus Applicable Sales Tax (see chart at right)	
			Plus Shipping & Handling (see chart at right)	
			TOTAL:	

Shipping & Handling:
If your subtotal is:
$15.00 and under add $3.50
$15.01 to $30.00 add $5.25
$30.01 to $55.00 add $6.50
$55.01 to $75.00 add $7.75
$75.01 to $100.00 add $8.75
$100.01 and up add $9.75
Sales Tax
(CO 3%, DC 6%, FL 6%, GA 6%, IL 6.25%, MD 5%, MI 6%, NC 6%, TX 6.25%, VT 5%, VA 4.5%)